BADGE OF MADNESS

JAMES WILLWERTH

BADGE OF MADNESS

THE TRUE STORY OF A PSYCHOTIC COP

M Evans
Lanham • New York • Boulder • Toronto • Plymouth, UK

M. Evans
An imprint of The Rowman & Littlefield Publishing Group, Inc.
4501 Forbes Boulevard, Suite 200, Lanham, Maryland 20706
http://www.rlpgtrade.com

10 Thornbury Road, Plymouth PL6 7PP, United Kingdom

Distributed by National Book Network

British Library Cataloguing in Publication Information Available

Library of Congress Cataloging-in-Publication Data Available

ISBN 13: 978-1-59077-329-1 (pbk: alk. paper)

♾™ The paper used in this publication meets the minimum requirements of American National Standard for Information Sciences—Permanence of Paper for Printed Library Materials, ANSI/NISO Z39.48-1992.

Printed in the United States of America

For Fred and Mark Willwerth
For Ardis
And for the Kauer family

FOREWORD

I FIRST met Pete Bon Viso on a blustery December afternoon in 1974. He wore a gray suit, and I recall my strong impression of his coal-dark eyes and darker, drooping mustache. Somewhere in that memory, or my impressions of him in subsequent meetings, is a plumed wide-brimmed hat; and, of course, the gun.

He showed me the gun at my office late one night. When he pulled back his coat to reveal it, I suddenly looked at his face. "I'm *still* a cop," he was saying. His face seemed to fume, like dying charcoal, and now I had a sense of the journey we were about to take. It was not reassuring.

As this is written, I'm about to complete the second year of that odyssey and I'm often surprised to have gotten this far. For Pete is at war with himself; it was too easy to be caught in the crossfire. All along, I had a sense of picking my way through enemy territory as I searched for explanations, or simple proof of some of the story's more bizarre moments. He reacted almost violently to some things I turned up; on other occasions he talked to me in ways that brought him to tears. This is a story, admittedly, that will take the reader's imagination into unaccustomed areas. It has mirrors within mirrors, and I suspect that some of the images are lost forever. But it is a true story. The pieces of the puzzle are there.

I've written this story largely as Pete remembers it, taking my material from conversations started that wind-blown December day. There were other valuable sources: Pete's mother, Rose Bon Viso, his former wife, Helen, his lover, Marge Riley, cops from the Ninth Precinct who were close to him, childhood friends, newspaper clippings—and most important, the recollections of his former partner, Paul Rossi. Sadly, I did not have access to the New York City Police Department's account of what happened, since as a matter of policy, they do not make a cop's personal file public. It is an appropriate policy, I suppose, but one which leaves some questions of public responsibility unanswered—such as what the department might do to prevent a recurrence of the sort of tragedy which brought Pete Bon Viso down and might have hurt innocent people along the way.

One other point: except in the cases of Pete, Helen and Rose Bon Viso, all names in this book have been changed. Pete's friends and family wanted it that way. His story is still a frightening and embarrassing mystery to them.

Ideally, that mystery should be resolved. Yet the questions of *why* continue to haunt everyone involved. There are explanations, which I think will be apparent to a careful reader of this book. It happens that mental illness interests me personally. It has disrupted my own family life, and I have begun to realize that I have a personal interest in writing about it. But I am a writer, not a trained analyst. It would be inappropriate for me to attempt to explain Pete Bon Viso in medical terms. He is no one's patient; he refuses to be. His nightmare is the story. And given that, I have taken the reader through it in a way that should reveal as much about Pete as I know. I freely admit, of course, that there were times during the last two years when I wondered if I knew him at all.

J.K.W., New York City

BADGE OF MADNESS

CHAPTER 1

COPIAGUE, Long Island: a rain-spattered spring day in 1974. The long block called "Eastgate," lined snugly with simple tract homes, had a mask of moderately resolved ambition. It was an hour's drive from the dirt and tension of Manhattan; many of its residents, new immigrants from the larger city, would have preferred even greater distance. A light breeze swept off a broad area of adjoining schoolyards where the block ended, washing through young trees, bending geraniums and ivy in the window boxes and small gardens.

This was a dream street, usually an easy and comfortable place, caught impatiently in the wake of the cold season. The weather had kept the children inside too long. Easter Sunday had come and gone, and the skies were still cloaked in a lion's winter mane, forcing husbands home through unseasonable storms. It was a spring that suggested mythic discontent—nature's furies loosed, dark clouds overhead, grey mist at night.

In another era Eastgate's neighbors might have known why.

For strange trouble had come to their community. A New York City policeman living with his guns and his family at the far end of the block was caught in some kind of fearful crisis. There had been reports of a strange gun battle, then rumors of an attempt to murder a state official. The papers talked of stolen heroin, police corruption, rogue cops. The headlines were huge; the policeman was at the center of the scandal.

And from his house came only silence. He was known to be inside, stalking about as if possessed.

Nestled against the schoolyards, the policeman's house seemed tall in the fading light. It was swollen at the top by a dormer addition, a symbol of the cop's ambition. He'd built the addition evenings after work and in spare weekends with the help of his friends, and on this particular night the new master bedroom was already completed; the adjoining bathroom's essential plumbing newly installed.

But the work had stopped with the bathroom unfinished. It remained a space of exposed plaster board and random pipe fittings—a place where he loitered when he wanted to be alone, perhaps to consider the irony of his life.

His name was Pete Bon Viso. He was 25, and the house was his pride and accomplishment. Two years earlier, he'd bought it—in shambles, deserted, long foreclosed—as th nugget of his dream of escaping an urban poor past. Pete and his equally city-bred wife, Helen, had renovated and furnished the house to fulfill their choicest fantasies. The pine-paneled living room looked as though they had run amok in an airport novelty shop. One wall featured a mass-produced print of a rocky, surf-lashed seashore. The room itself swarmed with gadgetry: toy trains, a Federal eagle over the fireplace, antique pistol wine bottles, a Bavarian drinking stein, a tank filled with decorative feathers, countless other knickknacks. Sitting on the beige corduroy sofa planted in deep green wall-to-wall carpeting, a visitor might look first toward the rear of the house. In a rambling space encompassing two former bedrooms was the new recreation room: vinyl-asbestos slate-look tiles, Spanish Oak false ceiling beams against a white stucco ceiling, *two* wine racks, a dart board, a huge walnut paneled bar with an ice bucket shaped like a knight's helmet. And, behind the bar, scores of framed pictures—friends and relatives smiling, showing off, sitting at night club tables, clinking glasses, standing at family gatherings, awkward in the camera's eye but happy, even proud.

The young cop, in turn, was proud of all he had put together. The house was his plumage, his place in the American dream.

At dinner's end this night, curly-haired Billy Bon Viso, five months old, lay in his bassinet, gurgling and groping for his toys. The boy's room, designed and constructed by his father, had red burlap-covered walls with wooden lattice work hiding its seams. Pete had put Billy's white crib in the corner, a small chair next to it, a blue crushed-velvet rug on the floor. Next, he'd thumbtacked cardboard cutouts of Disney characters onto the burlap: Mickey Mouse,

Goofy, Donald Duck, Snow White. He'd put a wind-up mobile over the crib, and then he had framed Billy's birth certificate and hung it. A small comic policeman stood on the dresser and held a stop sign. The room's colors were red, white and blue. Pete wanted his son to be an all-American kid.

By late evening, after the long day's rain, a thick mist rose. It settled over the block in a wet, tubercular breath, cutting off contact with the outside world. Patches of yellow hung from the street lamps, and the houses' lights peered like swollen eyes into the darkness.

Pete Bon Viso had spent the day on the living room floor, propped up by a mock leopard-skin pillow, sheltered by a comforter, bare-chested and without shoes. He'd risen at noon, eaten listlessly, then checked the basketball scores, even though he wasn't betting basketball this year. He searched next for the daily pari-mutuel number and checked yesterday's triple for the trotters, a habit more than anything else. He didn't like the horses that much, either.

He had said little to Helen as he idled and fidgeted, turning the newspaper's pages without seeing them. In mid-afternoon Pete and Helen had watched a detective movie on television. Afterward, he wandered into the bathroom to wash his hands, re-comb his hair and stare at his unshaven, lately chalky face. When Helen asked about his gloom, he talked vaguely of "the pressure." Nothing more.

Bon Viso, in Italian, means "good vision"—more loosely translated, "good face." Pete's full name was Peter John Bon Viso, and his face was a collection of striking features:

bushy eyebrows joined over a large Roman nose, drooping mustache, black cat's eyes. Above all, the large anxious eyes, both predatory and frightened. The face also accommodated a hotbed of moods. He could be a clowning street kid, a protective father radiating warmth and affection, a loving husband. But without warning, he might plummet into a powerful depression, wallowing for hours in bottomless sadness and silence. And the eyes, surfacing in the midst of it, would betray the reason.

It was the fear. Sometimes it fairly raged in him. It made his face flow and fume up like a skillet left too long over a fire. Most of the time, sometimes with great pain, he kept the fear sputtering just below the surface, where it gnawed viciously at him. He lived with this fear every moment of his life: in the streets, where he often sensed danger; at the gambling tables, when he faced major losses. At any time, his temperature might rise perceptibly at the thought of rejection by loved ones, or the ridicule of a vague public. Always, it was important to him to hide this. Sometimes he covered his passion with laughter and pranks. Failing that, he assumed a mask of silence, which meant the fire was rising.

Tonight, Pete's face carried that desperate silence again, a blankness devoid of all laughter.

For Victorio Sanchez was coming—again. Somewhere in a dark well of feelings, Pete knew this. He knew that the man was coming to kill him, even though the act made no sense to him. He did not know when Sanchez would come, but he knew it would be soon, and he knew he must fight. He had an arsenal waiting: two hunting rifles, a twelve-gauge shotgun, three handguns, a sawed-off shotgun. And he had hundreds of rounds of ammunition stored in strategic places around the house.

No one had phoned today. A telephone was Pete Bon Viso's lifeline. Telephones rang for *him*. It was a thing of his. He liked making calls, and he liked getting them. Each day of his life, he called nearly everyone he knew, just to connect. He had to be sure that things were in place, and that he was abreast of any changes.

But today the phone was not used. Happily, of course, there were none of the frightening calls: slow, heavy breathing . . . and no voice. They'd scared Helen so badly that Pete had changed the telephone number. But the comforting calls were missing as well.

Paul hadn't called.

No one mattered as much in his life as Paul Rossi, his partner. Paul lived in Port Jefferson now, an hour's drive toward the far end of the island. A year earlier, Paul and his wife, Catherine, had lived three houses away, connected not only by regular telephone, but by a military "batphone" whose wire was strung over fences and through trees so that the two could talk any time of the day or night without mounting up message units. The batphone's flat bell sounded constantly; the two cops talked like teenagers. They had gone on extended "dump runs" together, usually to a bar to drink and play pool. They had driven to the precinct together, worked as partners on the same shift and often stayed at Pete's mother's house between back-to-back shifts, keeping exclusive company for as long as 36 hours before returning to their wives.

For nearly three years, they had lived like brothers,

which they often seemed to be. But today Paul had not called. And Pete, in his depressed, almost vacuous state of apprehension, had no energy to pick up the phone himself.

Remarkably, Rose Bon Viso, Pete's mother, had not called either. She was 62, widowed four years, still living in a cramped city-subsidized flat where she and Pete's father Bill Bon Viso, had raised Pete and his sisters. She had been badly deformed in childhood by a severe hip fracture complicated by tuberculosis. Yet despite her difficulties, she refused welfare and worked nights as a cleaning woman. By day, she kept house with a vengeful eye for small details, moving about with a heaving, twisted step. She called Pete and Helen almost every day, particularly now that she had a grandson. But today she hadn't called.

In the kitchen, Helen Bon Viso, the Polish-descended daughter of two generations of cops, puttered about, finished the dishes, listening for sounds of Billy over the television's chatter. She was a comely woman, with a lean, girlish figure, eyes still filled with mischief. She liked to wear colorful blouses and styled jeans, and they looked good with her dark hair and slim figure. She had a button nose, and the nose had a pugnacious turn to it, as if she remembered the mischief and trouble of her childhood.

Until recently, Helen's adult life had been sublimely happy. Pete was her high school love. He'd told her long before she dared believe it that they would have a baby and a nice house. And five years of marriage had given her those dreams. Sometimes they seemed almost fantasies when contrasted with her painful childhood: her three-year-old brother's death, officially pneumonia but actually caused by a punctured lung—the result of a drunken beating by her father, who died soon afterward of a heart attack. And the family's continuing poverty. Helen's mother, Mary, the self-reliant daughter of Russian and Polish immigrants, had wrestled with this legacy all her adult life, enduring two emotional breakdowns through a succession of boyfriends and a second husband whom Helen neither liked nor understood.

Helen could say with absolute conviction that her marriage to Pete had given her the finest hours of her life, a life made even happier by the birth and recent christening of her baby. Yet now her husband was in serious trouble, and she didn't know why, or what it would soon mean to her life.

That night, in a feeble attempt to liven things up, Pete had smoked a long black C.W. Perkins Ambassador from his "private" collection made by a Lower East Side tobacconist. "They're cheap and they stink like a bastard," he'd once laughed when in a better mood, "but they look good." The cigar didn't make up for the fact that the phone was silent.

A full moon filled the backyard with pale light, pushing through the mist like a ship's beacon. Pete's yard, still slightly rural, was large for a tract home. It was backed by a tall Cyclone fence separating it from the tarred playground used by one of the schools, and to the right, his land sloped evenly across thick grass to a low metal fence marking a neighbor's property. To the near left, the remnant of a small stream flowed from beside his house into a wooded area.

The township would soon fill in the stream, but for now

the area had a sense of gothic woodland. A twisted old weeping willow's branches fell to the water's edge in the moonlight.

An immense woodpile—a tall stack of oak and elm logs cut by Pete the previous year—stood about 75 feet from the patio on the other side of the stream, beyond the weeping willow. Another tree, a tall elm, stood beside it, just now beginning to add spring buds to its stark winter skeleton.

Pete emerged from the breezeway with Bruno, a wet-eyed mutt with terrier and cocker spaniel ancestors, prancing ahead. The moon's light was strong, so Pete did not turn on his floodlights. Nor did he bring his guns, which was unusual.

He heard the first noise, an odd rustling, when the dog was at the far end of the yard. Pete froze—listening, staring into the darkness.

He knew someone was behind the stack of logs.

He strained to see through the mist and moonlight, feeling sharp needles of ice behind his eyes. Then he whistled softly for the dog, which trotted obediently into the house. Pete turned abruptly on his heels and walked into the breezeway, reaching for the 12-gauge shotgun behind the door. He broke the gun to be sure that a shell was inside, then reached for more cartridges and stuffed them into his pocket, silent as the fear worked on him. He crossed the patio and walked slowly toward the wooded area. The twisted weeping willow stood to his left, framed by a cloudy moon.

He found Sanchez in the moonlight.

Pete saw the gunman rise from behind the dark logpile

—a short thick Hispanic man with closely cropped hair and hot eyes, his mouth angrily twisted. In the half-second it took Pete to walk across the patio and onto the grass—Pete was 30 feet from the woodpile now—Sanchez became fully visible from the waist up, standing with the moon behind him, waiting with his gun poised at his side.

It was the same gun, a black .38 caliber pistol with an evil snout fully six inches long. As Pete approached, Sanchez seemed content to let it hang in his right hand, as though he would simply draw and fire once. He said nothing; it was understood why he was there.

A heartbeat passed in silence. Pete suddenly raised his gun and aimed it, catching Sanchez by surprise. The gunman broke and ran in short, jerky motions toward the stream.

Blam!

The thunder of Pete's discharge rumbled across the schoolyard and slammed against the buildings, echoing back.

A clean *miss*. Pete couldn't believe he had missed at 30 feet! In a rush of blood, rage replaced his fear. Sidestepping furiously as Sanchez sprinted to the left, Pete broke open the gun again, shoved another shell into it and took aim, gunsight slightly ahead of his fleeing target as a hunter might draw down on a prize mallard.

The report echoed again. Sanchez's trenchcoat billowed like a raincloud as he leaped the streambed and rushed headlong for the metal fence.

Pete nearly screamed, cursing loudly as he released the safety and broke open the gun to drop the smoking shell. He sidestepped desperately to get in position for a last shot.

He jammed a third shell into the hot chamber and raised the gun.

This time the shot sounded curiously hollow, echoing again across the schoolyard but falling into empty space. Sanchez was gone. He'd cleared the fence in a single short-legged leap, and he was part of the night now, running swiftly toward a car somewhere in the distance.

Returning to the house, Pete shook violently, his face as grey as the night.

"Pete!" Helen shouted, running to the door. "Pete!"

"He's still around." Pete stared at the ground morosely. Something seemed caught in his throat. "I knew I didn't get him. I *knew* it."

It was all too strange, almost . . . unreal. Five days earlier, Pete had been trapped in a dark Manhattan hallway in a terrifying gun battle with Victorio Sanchez, 33, a heroin addict, sometime gunman and drug dealer from New York's Lower East Side. In the end, because he was faster —because he was more frightened—Pete had fired ten times at Sanchez, blasting as if the hounds of hell were loosed in the darkness. And Pete had seen his assailant fall. He had seen him twist and bleed and grow silent.

He had seen him die. He was convinced of it.

But two days after the fight, Pete was suspended from the New York City police force while newspaper headlines speculated on a major police scandal. And tonight, three days after the suspension, Sanchez had come alive and invaded his home for the second time.

Pete was lost in a nightmare of horror and confusion. Nothing in his life or police career had prepared him for this.

CHAPTER 2

In May of 1969, as the Ninth Precinct's day shift was about to begin, an oddly half-ancient young cop approached the lieutenant sitting at the precinct desk. The cop saluted and asked for a memo book, the 50-page notebook that is the tableau for everything official a New York City patrolman does—call-ins, routine neighborhood business, arrests, notations of stolen property. The desk officer normally opens each man's book by signing his name and the day's date across the top of the first page—and closes the old one by signing it out.

"Where's the old book?" the lieutenant said without looking up.

"I don't have one, sir."

"Whaddya mean?" The lieutenant was looking at Pete now.

"This is my first day here."

"Oh."

And the lieutenant looked at the probationary patrolman carefully. Something about him was hard to figure. Somehow he looked older.

That previous night, Pete had taken his shiny new holster and its leather accessories and had beaten them into premature old age with his nightstick. He'd darkened his shield with soft pencil lead and whacked it with the stick to dent the numerals. He'd also squeezed and rumpled his hat and generally worked on his uniform to add six months of wear and tear. The other cops in the precinct might see through his disguise, he reasoned, but it would work in the streets.

Today, he was given patrol post 47-48. He had an 11 A.M. meal break, followed by a noon reassignment to special post seven, a church on St. Mark's Place troubled by vandals. Pete also had an "O-1" ring, which meant he should call the stationhouse at one minute past each hour in case they had something to tell him.

A city guidebook might have called his new beat "colorful." For the Lower East Side's streets were a diverse patchwork of life styles and ethnic influences. In the hot months the people spilled into them like water rushing from a thousand fire hydrants—kids playing handball against the sides of buildings, winos at each corner with their sticky bottles, hustlers scheming, ladies strutting. The ice cream man rang his chimes and offered sweet rewards for small change; wash fluttered out of tenement windows, men with dice and dollar bills crouched in doorways, junkies nodded in hallways, and everyone else seemed to be sitting on the stoops drinking from bottles encased in brown paper or leaning out of windows watching the parade below. It seemed like one big party to Pete.

That was the coin's shiny side. Behind the color was a festering culture of poverty. Its twin gods were death and madness, attended on a regal garbage heap by a cacophony of gruesome subalterns who dealt in hunger, poverty, disease and rejection. Along the avenues that Pete would walk, the wretched spirits flew from curb to grimy street-corner in company with beggars, winos, drug addicts, and cheap hustlers, all trying to "get over" for another day. The spirits claimed the poor, the hungry, the afflicted—mostly blacks and Puerto Ricans now.

Today's post covered four blocks of Second Avenue between Fourth Street and St. Mark's Place. The area had been a major pop-culture scene when hippies and runaway children dominated it during the Sixties, but by 1969 the street had been retaken by merchants and a population of relatively stable middle-class dropouts.

Second Avenue was, in fact, a sort of middle ground for the Ninth, which in turn was known to be one of the city's roughest precincts. The Ninth was small, covering less than one square mile of lower Manhattan, starting north at 14th Street, stretching south to Houston Street, west to Broadway and east to the river at Manhattan's edge. Cheap housing and an immigrant tradition had made it a haven—and often an urban hell—for poor people.

The census said that more than 80,000 people lived in the Ninth, about half of them white (that number was dropping fast), the rest black, Puerto Rican and Chinese. Puerto Ricans were the non-white majority, outnumbering the blacks two to one. One Ninth Precinct landmark was the Bowery, home to a desperately sad, seemingly endless parade of derelicts, winos and the mentally ill. Pete's colleagues called them "skells," short for skeleton, and "psychos"—meaning those who had to be taken screaming, bleeding or unconscious to Bellevue.

The Ninth headquarters was a six-story building on East Fifth Street between First and Second Avenues, built in 1912. Marked by a long flagpole reaching toward Fifth Street like an arm in a plaster cast, the command post resembled an old fortress, which in spiritual terms it was. For crime in New York City—violent street crime, the kind that society worried about—was the province of the poor. The poor were the criminals, and, more often than not, the victims.

So the larger society, mindful of its civic responsibilities, had erected fortresses at strategic locations around the city to monitor, and sometimes interfere with the troubles that poor people in places like the Lower East Side got into. The men at the fort were local soldiers paid to keep the civic order, variously defined by themselves as "protecting the people," taking "bad guys" off the streets, or simply keeping the lid on. The cops measured themselves accordingly. Status was accrued through arrests, *not* by the babies delivered, friends made (unless they happened to be informers), or family disputes settled. The measure of a cop like Pete Bon Viso would be in how well he could "catch." It was that simple.

And so on that half-warm spring day, newly minted (but carefully scuffed up) New York City patrolman Peter Bon Viso, 21, walked along Second Avenue among the kids, businessmen and hippies and made his phone calls to the fortress at precisely one minute after every hour. He took his meal at 11 A.M., reported after that to Special Post Num ber Seven, an old deserted Roman Catholic Church, and proceeded to stand on the corner contemplating the gathering warmth of the afternoon and the dignity and fascination of his new position in life.

He noticed a middle-aged, somewhat unkempt woman, chubby and short, walking across the street in his direction with two large dogs in tow. She had gray hair, haphazardly combed, and baggy, bloodshot eyes which locked hard into his.

"Hi, officer."

"Hello, miss." (A bit of gallantry never hurt.)

"You're new here?"

"Yes." All of Pete's careful work gone to waste. "How did you know that?"

"You know me?" the woman asked mysteriously.

"No." Pete was genuinely perplexed.

"Well, my name is Ruthie," she smiled.

And suddenly he felt her hand between his legs. She held his genitals tightly. Pete blushed tomato red, flailed around, reaching for his nightstick, thinking he'd knock her down or slap her on the head or *something*. But she stood back from him laughing low and happy. Then she turned on her heel, pulling the dogs. "See you around," she laughed, and Pete Bon Viso, naked in front of the public he was sworn to protect, scurried behind the church he was supposed to be guarding. The rest of the day was mercifully uneventful.

Paul Rossi spent his first night in the Ninth standing a freezing, and he thought unnecessary, Christmas Eve watch. He thought about rum punch, and he thought about his wife and kids. Other Christmases had been better; he remembered all of them that night.

He was a shy, skinny kid—"skinny as a goddam toothpick"—whose family had moved from Brooklyn to a rural part of Long Island when he was eight. His father, John Rossi, had worked at two jobs to get the family into the suburbs, the primary one as a trackwalker for the Metropolitan Transit Authority. Paul admired his father boundlessly. He remembered him as a huge and happy man, full of laughter with his shiny black hair parted cleanly on the left. John Rossi smoked thick smelly cigars as he worked around the house or watched cowboy movies on television. In some ways, he was an old-world version of Pete Bon Viso; Paul knew it instinctively.

Paul graduated from high school at 17 and announced that he planned to join the Marines and go to Vietnam. But John Rossi chomped tightly on his cigar and refused to sign the papers, telling his son in no uncertain terms to get a job and *think* about his life. Paul joined the Air National Guard and took the New York City police test instead.

"I wanted to do something exciting," he explained later. "I *liked* excitement." He dreamed, too, of becoming a Hollywood stunt man.

By this time he was a slightly reserved young man with soft dark hair and a handsome boyish face. The job would bring enormous changes in his life. "I grew up as a suburban kid, practically a country kid," he said once. "I never saw a prostitute, a junkie, a weirdo anything like that. You just didn't see things like that on Long Island. At night people sat out in front of their houses. They talked, the kids played in the yards. It was nice."

In 1967, John Rossi's heart failed. It was a wintry December day on the Manhattan Bridge; he was dead before the ambulance arrived. "I'm *still* crushed about it," Paul says now. Pete Bon Viso's life would soon be similarly shattered, helping to form a strong bond between the two men.

After high school, Paul worked briefly as an apprentice machinist and in 1968 married his high school girlfriend, Catherine Biaggi, a pouty, dark-haired coed who at 17 had asked about his plans. "I'm going where the sun is shining and the surf is big," Paul had boasted. They were married when Catherine graduated from nursing school.

Paul went into the department with a solid "Wyatt Earp complex." He lost it within the year. "I thought it would be great being a cop," he said later. "I didn't think there was such a thing as corruption. You just caught the bad guys, and they went to jail like on television. I wanted to be a real crusader." The streets failed to live up to his vision.

His first arrest was something less than High Noon.

At 3 A.M. on a late tour during his trainee period, Paul passed a greasy spoon at Broadway and 50th Street and heard a commotion in the back room. A huge black man and a smaller white man seemed to be fighting. A robbery? Paul charged inside.

He stepped squarely into a mop bucket on wheels.

Slipping and sliding, badly stuck, he identified himself

with as much dignity as he could muster. The black man, who turned out to be the cook, fled to the front counter. The white man reached up and grabbed Paul's necktie, nearly choking him. Paul struggled, splashing soapy water on the floor.

The tie-holder, apparently drunk, seemed unimpressed by Paul's uniform, badge or gun. Paul hit him on the shoulder with his night stick "just like they showed me in the Academy." The man didn't move.

Paul tried another Academy technique. Steadying himself in the wobbly bucket, by now nearly empty of water, he held both ends of the night stick and used it to pin the man against the wall. Success. His opponent began to speak.

"Take the nightstick away."

"Not until you calm down."

"Then *I'll* take the nightstick away from *you*," the man answered. And he did. Patrolman Paul Rossi was suddenly very frightened.

Reinforcements arrived. Two cops rushed through the door and piled on top of the man. Paul threw his arms around his tormentor, catching him in a tight headlock. But the man threw off the other cops and lifted Paul off the floor, mop bucket and all, dropping him like a soggy basketball in a nearby sink. Superior numbers finally prevailed when one of the cops got his nightstick around the man's neck and pulled sharply, closing off his windpipe. The man passed out while Paul watched helplessly from his new perch, shaking a wet leg.

The "perpetrator" got ten days in jail, and Paul got free

coffee and eggs from the cook who was grateful for his
deliverance. And Wyatt Earp was on his way to becoming
a dim memory.

Five weeks after Paul had put on his probationary uniform, Martin Luther King was murdered in Memphis,
setting off riots in a number of major American cities.
Paul spent seven months after that standing in front of
midtown Manhattan stores to prevent broken windows.

"I was trying hard to believe that someone wasn't paying
somebody else to have me there," he recalled later. "That
was my first real sour note. I was ready for riots. I was
ready to be in there. And here I was standing in front of
those stupid windows, doing nothing."

In the winter of 1968, disillusioned with his new career,
Paul returned to the Police Academy for reassignment. He
was eventually sent to the Ninth, working mostly foot
patrols. Pete joined the precinct six months later.

"I thought he was a hairbag, a typical city hairbag," Paul
remembered, finding himself briefly fooled by Pete's disguise. A "hairbag" is an old-timer in cop language, a somewhat pejorative term for someone who shows his age. Paul
also noticed that Pete rarely caught a walking post.

"Pete knew everybody's name. He looked older. He
looked like he'd been on the job ten years. And he always
rode in cars." Eventually Paul realized that Pete rode because he "bought someone a hat"—Pete bribed the people
who made out the schedules with liquor and five dollar
bills. He noticed, too, that Pete was possessed of a particular charm: like Paul's father, he could *talk* to people,
whether bosses or street corner hustlers. Ultimately, Pete's

surface charm—and Paul's lack of it—led people to think of Pete as the "good guy" in the partnership. Paul was withdrawn and cool with strangers, also fast-tempered. He was the "bad guy," a role he accepted with casual indifference.

"It didn't bother me," he says. "They teach in the Police Academy that you should use whatever force is necessary to arrest a person who is resisting. If someone started trouble with me, I gave it right back. I wasn't out there to be a whipping post."

Pete, of course, was no Little Boy Blue. He was a former street kid well practiced with his fists and his club. When angry, he was Paul's match for brutality any time. "I couldn't work in a middle-class neighborhood," Pete once said. "When someone shouts at me, I shout back. When someone hits me, I hit back. That's what people understand in poor neighborhoods. I was raised in one." He paused and shrugged at this point. "I get angry just like they do. A uniform doesn't make you a saint."

But Pete preferred to talk. Something held his passion. "I figure if a guy's getting arrested, he's got trouble," he said. "I give him the benefit of the doubt." It was an instinct that Paul believes caused his friend's crisis with Victorio Sanchez. "He should have blown that fucking guy away," Paul has said many times.

"You see cops on TV," Jerry Bono, an early partner, remembers, "and Pete was like that. Most cops aren't, you know. They just do a job. For Pete, it was *the* job."

Jerry Bono comes out of Flatbush, where he got into a fair amount of trouble growing up. He is a lean man with powerful shoulders and big hands. As a teenager, he studied karate, and at 16 he was arrested for using his well-educated hands, which were considered weapons, on another high school kid. A judge advised him to join the Army. Eventually he took the New York City police test, passed it, and appeared before a department board to argue successfully that the karate incident belonged to his foolish childhood. Police work soon became his consuming passion.

During his rookie days, Jerry worked regularly with either Pete or Paul. Five years later, when Pete was a friendly but fading memory, Jerry had made Detective Third Grade, and he lived in a small house on Staten Island. But in many ways, he remained a street kid like Pete. He liked action. Movement mattered enormously to him, and conflict was sweet. He was having a great ride.

"Pete was right as a cop," Jerry remembers now. "If he could make a collar five minutes before the shift ended, he did. If he hadda park the radio car and hide for half an hour to make the collar, he would. If the incident called for going into a building, he didn't back off and call for assistance while the guy got away. He went *in*."

Jerry hunches forward.

"If it's in you, it's everything. It's in me, and it was in him. He wasn't good at the tests, but he knew the streets. He'd do crazy things. It was nothing to see him in a pool room shooting pool with some guys. You can get in trouble for that, but it's also how you find out things, you know?"

On Avenue A one night, Pete and Jerry saw a white man struggling with two blacks. It was a slushy winter night, and as they started toward the fight, the white man jumped away and ran down 11th Street.

"That motherfucker robbed us," one of the black men wailed.

Pete charged down the block with Jerry close behind. "I grabbed him at the corner of 12th Street," Pete recalled, "and I smacked him in the face. I always smacked guys, I don't know why. He fell down and Jerry ran up and sorta kicked him. We were working him over when he yells the other two guys robbed him. We looked down at him like he was making a joke or something."

The man had neither weapons nor money, and he was bleeding from an obvious knife wound.

"What'd you run for?" Pete asked in exasperation.

"I was scared."

And Pete and Jerry suddenly looked at each other, and then down the street. The men were gone. Cursing, they wrote up the victim's robberv complaint and began looking for the muggers.

A few hours later, they spotted someone on Fourth Street.

The man kept walking, and when they called to him he walked faster. They finally caught up with him and pushed him into a hallway.

The man started to scream. He pushed Pete and tried to run.

"I grabbed him by his Afro, and I started bringing his face down into my knee, and Jerry swung his nightstick." Pete chuckled at the memory. "And Jerry hit *me* on the hand. I screamed and opened my hand and the guy broke free. He was out the door and gone."

And they returned to the precinct house in fury and

amusement, empty-handed. "It's a crazy job," Jerry observed later. "You don't get the action like on the TV shows most of the time. But for eight hours you do see things that ordinary people don't see. Like the time we pushed open a door and a dead woman's face peeled right off on it. It's horrible, but it's interesting, you know?"

Pete loved it all. Driving on Avenue A with Jerry one night in 1971, he saw a man slumped over a car's steering wheel. Pete approached the car from the street side, Jerry the opposite. The man came alive and looked at Pete. He had a gun.

"Freeze!" Jerry yelled, pointing his revolver through the window.

Jerry happened to be "catching"—looking for an arrest —so he took the case. At the precinct, Pete remembered that they hadn't fully searched the man's car, and he drove back to it. On the way he heard a 14th Street burglary-in-progress call. He arrived at a shoe store in time to meet a young junkie carrying 12 boxes of shoes out the door. Pete stopped him at gunpoint, searched and handcuffed him and asked the sector cops who arrived a few minutes later if they wanted the arrest. Nobody was catching, so Pete took it: another mark on his scorecard, another day in court.

As it turned out, the car he went back to check was empty.

He was a gung-ho cop and an intense booster of the brotherhood. "I gotta *be* there if another cop is in trouble," he would say. "Any cop, it doesn't matter who." It was a common feeling, born of a shared notion among cops that they are at the barricades; and that no one really understands this. Pete had brothers now. He'd wanted them since childhood.

And for now, he was too young, too eager, to be frightened. But like anyone else, Pete did think of death. He rehearsed each situation as he sped toward it. On a burglary run, he looked at the building in his mind's eye, locating the building's alley and back entrance, making his decisions about where to go, whether to break his gun or use a flashlight. At these times he planned the next fifteen minutes of his life as carefully as he planned the following year.

He was assigned one night to the car of an overweight, red-faced fortyish cop. The older man planned to retire and collect his pension in a year. He was thinking about little else.

A "shots fired" call came in, giving an address on Fifth Street between Avenues C and D, a block of abandoned buildings. The older cop, a veteran of more than 12 years in the precinct, sped toward Fifth Street and made a wrong turn that dead-ended a block later in a school yard.

"How could I have made that mistake?" he said sheepishly.

Pete curled his upper lip in disgust in the darkness.

Other cops were in control by the time they arrived. "It got to the point where nobody wanted to work with this guy," Pete remembered later. "If there was trouble, nobody expected to see him."

In that moment of recollection, Pete stopped, puzzled. His face became briefly blank with hidden thoughts. "When I think about it now," he shrugged suddenly, "I guess I couldn't blame him."

The Ninth had 20 squadrons, and Pete and Paul generally worked the same shift. They talked cautiously at first. But a precinct house is like a dormitory; the sense of shelter it gives can lead to intense relationships. Cops tend to trust other cops and no one else. And in time these friendships can become so intense they resemble love affairs. It happened to Pete and Paul. Pete soon came to believe he would put no other human being before his partner; not his wife, not his mother.

They began to drink together at Cal's, a dark low-ceilinged bar several doors west. Cal, a wise old bullfrog with big eyes and a leathery face poured the drinks and there was a pool table in back. It was a place to tell the day's war stories, talk of troubles at home, beef about the bosses. Bare wooden tables and chairs sat forlornly about. The ambiance was early waterfront, at best.

"Pete always had funny stories to tell," Paul remembered. "Bullshit, but funny. It was easy. I liked spending time with him." And soon they asked for sector car assignments together.

For any cop, the streets have a shadowy texture. Eight hours riding in a radio car can be insufferably dull: gray, ghostly, almost lifeless. Long hours of cruising to the background of a buzzing, squawking radio age a man. In winter, the cold cuts through his clothing; the summer humidity makes his skin itch and fester under a sweat-soaked uniform. He seems to be drifting through space. He remembers he should be studying for the sergeant's test, and as the years go by, he looks down at his folded-over paunch and curses himself.

If he doesn't pass the sergeant's test, or lacks a "hook" (a sponsor in the ranks) to help him become a detective, he'll spend 20 years cruising the streets literally looking for trouble to make the time pass—or come to hope for boredom.

For the shadows might also contain a dark, unpredictable time lapse, that moment of bad luck. Maybe a psychotic will stick a knife in him without warning. It happened in the Ninth in 1970. Perhaps he'll be the Black Liberation Army's next "political statement." That happened to patrolmen Gregory Foster and Rocco Laurie in 1972 in the Ninth. Or his bad luck might be more conventional. He'll catch a bullet in the middle of a liquor store robbery, or a knife while attempting to stop a drunken family fight.

It gives a man too much to think about as he rides. He'll try to avoid thinking, aiming his imagination elsewhere: girls and gambling, vacations, his kids. But this is momentary respite. Death on a ghetto beat is too close.

As close as Nodges Bar on St. Mark's Place. Pete and Paul were in separate cars that night, and when Pete arrived the robbers had run, leaving a blood-stained house. Nodges' employees and customers lay about like overturned mannequins, each killed by one shot in the heart or between the eyes. The bar looked as though someone had gone crazy in a wax museum. Pete found bodies all over the floor, human beings so suddenly dead they retained wide-eyed faces of shock.

The bartender was on his back. He held a small billie in one hand; his face had congealed into an expression of furious disbelief. The bar had been robbed before. The bartender's patience with thieves was known to be short.

Moments later Pete and the other cops found an old woman in back. She lay on a small cot, and her crutches had fallen to the floor. She owned Nodges Bar; she'd been shot once in the head. She was known to be crippled, and she could not have run away. An old fat woman in front was slightly alive. Pete drove her to Bellevue, lights and siren screaming. Paul arrived with the bar's other survivor, an old man. The doctors cut open the old man's chest, but the heart massage didn't work, and he died. And then the woman died, too.

It was an exchange of eight lives for whatever cash the register held.

Pete and Paul watched Don Bennett walk toward his Tasty Bread truck knowing he was right for the part: a perfect victim. Bennett was a short man, frail, traveling on spindly legs. He looked frightened.

If I was a criminal he's somebody *I'd* rip off, Pete thought. It was the summer of 1972.

The Lower East Side had lately suffered a rash of delivery truck robberies. Men with knives were jumping on board the puffed out trucks carrying Tasty Bread and Diet Rite Cola and forcing the drivers to give up their day's receipts. Bon Viso and Rossi, a tight partnership by now, had been assigned to do something about it.

They felt that a department car would be noticed, so they used Paul's Volkswagen, driving to a supermarket at Fourth Street and Avenue A where the delivery trucks made their earliest runs. They talked to the drivers, saying they'd be nearby most of the day. The delivery men were nervous enough as it was.

They'd planned to watch other trucks, but Don Bennett's fear pulled at them. They followed him most of the morning, keeping sandwiches and beer in the car. They had been drinking the night before. Paul drank soda to clear his head, Pete got right into the beer.

Don Bennett began carrying trays of bread in and out of the bodegas. Pete and Paul passed him on Avenue D between Fourth and Fifth Streets about 12:30, turning into Fourth Street where they parked the Volkswagen in order to watch him further. Pete left the car, carrying his beer in one hand, and walked across the avenue for a better view.

The driver returned to his truck after finishing the block's deliveries, then started a U-turn to go south. His turnaround was cramped by parked cars, so he negotiated the half circle in two parts, stopping the truck just short of one car and shifting gears to back up.

Pete saw a black man jump into the open door on Bennett's passenger side. Two men followed him. Pete's chest thumped loudly and he swallowed hard. He dropped his beer can on the sidewalk with a clatter and grabbed his gun, fishing in his side pocket for his shield. He ran toward the truck. From the Volkswagen, Paul saw one of the bandits put a knife to Don Bennett's throat. Paul jumped from his car and broke into a run.

Pete and Paul met in hurried confusion at the truck's passenger door and pushed their guns inside it, pointing them two-handed at the three surprised men.

"Police! Get out of the truck! Hands in the air!"

One man, who seemed high or drunk, stepped out of the Tasty Bread truck and walked past Pete as through he and Paul didn't exist. He started walking down Avenue D;

Pete grabbed him around the neck. A second man stepped down and stood beside the truck.

The third man, who carried the knife, came down. Everything exploded. The man Pete was holding began to struggle, and as he fought, the man standing beside the truck took flight. Now the man with the knife started to run. Paul jumped after him, yelling and running down the avenue. Then the man stopped, turned toward Paul and lunged at him with the knife.

Paul's bullet caught him squarely between the legs. The bandit flew backward onto the pavement, sitting down heavily and holding himself in the crotch as blood oozed out of his pants. He seemed stunned, and he tried to crawl away as Paul reached for him and dragged him back to the truck. The man looked at himself as though he could hardly believe what he saw. The gathering crowd was fully convinced that Paul had shot off the man's balls.

The crowd swelled with anger. In street clothes, Pete and Paul didn't look like cops, and the black and Puerto Rican crowd saw only that two white men had shot a black man. Pete was struggling again with the first man. Paul ran up and shoved the man's head into the bread truck and Pete brought his gun down on the man's head like a carpenter pounding a nail. The man stopped struggling now. Paul ran for his radio in the Volkswagen and called for emergency help. The crowd was closing in.

The crowd had become a sea of fists and catcalls. A wave of Spanish curses washed over Pete and Paul. Small stones began to rain down from a nearby rooftop. Pete felt a sharp stinging pain on one arm. He raised his revolver toward the roof and the stones stopped. A bottle sailed down and exploded like a bomb on the pavement.

Just as the crowd seemed about to overwhelm them, a Seventh precinct radio car appeared, followed by two from the Ninth. The crowd fell back, and Pete and Paul identified themselves. The cars escorted them to Bellevue, where surgeons stitched up Pete's opponent and found that the man Paul had shot wasn't in danger of losing anything after all.

Several months passed, and Pete and Paul spotted the man Paul had shot. He rode in a wheel chair, and stared at them hatefully. A few months later they saw him walking with a cane, limping badly, and this time he offered Paul his hand.

"That was some bullet you put in me."

"You're lucky it didn't go in your chest," Paul said matter-of-factly.

"No hard feelings, man."

It was an odd but common fact of life on Avenue C that criminals valued the friendship of cops who arrested them, as if they were somehow linked—as if the cop who had interrupted their lives, outsmarted or outfought them, was an authority figure, even a friend. At minimum the criminal was aiming to ensure his future safety, hoping that Pete and Paul would not make more trouble. An effective, if uneasy, truce resulted.

The shooting, of course, brought bosses, starting at the hospital. When bullets were fired, the department wanted to know why. Pete and Paul were required to tell the story half a dozen times; first to their sergeant, then to the division inspector and to several division captains, and finally to a boss from the borough command. Each time the bosses wondered out loud why the robber couldn't have been taken without bullets.

But the precinct bosses were happy, and the sergeant in charge of the neighborhood police teams, who would eventually die in a sidestreet gunfight after Pete had left the force, drove in on his day off to extend his congratulations. As was expected, their guns were taken for official inspection, and they were assigned to temporary office duty for the next two days.

It was customary to take a uniformed man from his beat after a shooting. The sooner the neighborhood forgot the incident, the department reasoned, the better for all concerned.

Pete and Paul were to be given service awards for the arrest. For now, they drank coffee and made phone calls in a headquarters office and then went home for three scheduled days off. Then they returned to Avenue C.

On that first day back, they arrested Victorio Sanchez. For Pete, it would all begin.

CHAPTER 3

THE men of the Ninth called them "Pretty" (Pete) and "Prettier" (Paul) and regarded them interchangeably. Pete liked that: he liked having a friend so close that other men mistook him for that friend.

They were known, also, as "Crazy Pete and Dirty Paul." Paul once broke a man's leg in the frenzy of trying to arrest him. A few weeks later they saw the man again, and they autographed his cast with their nicknames. They joked in Cal's that they were saving money for Paul's Swedish sex change operation. "After that," Paul laughed loudly over his beer, "I'm gonna give Pete the best blow jobs he's ever had!" Other cops stared wide-eyed and turned away, and the two laughed uproariously. An endless repertoire of crude humor seemed to be one of their strongest bonds.

Pete had been on the force for three years. Before meeting Paul, he'd gained a reputation as a solid, hard-working —and rather crazy—street cop. For he *liked* the street people. Sometimes he even danced with them. If the music was loud and they were dancing on the sidewalk or inside an open-door club, he boogied, too, fingers snapping, feet jumping. Maybe he'd been sent to silence them; but he'd dance first. On hot days, if his mood was right, he unbuttoned his blue shirt to show a hairy chest and the sparkle of chains and medals. Then he might shoot a little pool or drink some beer. He was no spit and polish cop, and he didn't think of himself that way.

Pete's past was buried with an old man he'd never met, a huge man with granite features and large charcoal eyes, haunted eyes that he passed through two generations to his grandson.

While he was young, John Valanti worked on the docks, as many first generation Italian immigrants did, hauling cargo, carrying weight the way a mule might. Yet it was never steady work, and he spent far too many days standing around the hall, "shaping" as it is called, because he didn't know the right people. As he grew older, the wasted days became more frequent, and finally he took a job as a street cleaner to support his wife and five children. He pushed a broom and cart for the rest of his working life, earning ten dollars a week.

He named his first daughter Rose. She was a tiny girl with spitfire eyes, a child who shook her fists at a world she didn't yet understand, crying and causing commotion in the beds and chairs she occupied. One day, during a tantrum, Rose shook loose from her highchair and fell squalling to the floor, breaking her hip badly. The fall was to mark her for the rest of her life. The family eventually sent her to a Catholic-supported caretaking hospital in Long Island, where she spent sixteen years among nuns, doctors and social workers. When she returned to her family on the Lower East Side as a teenager, she was as much of a stranger to the culture around her as John Valanti had been.

She was also sadly deformed. The hip fracture was complicated by tuberculosis which had most likely weakened the bones initially and now stunted their growth. In the end, Rose walked with her right leg bent and turned toward the other leg as if someone had kicked it viciously and she was unable to straighten it. Her right hip also seemed to be eaten away. A casual and unpitying look at this part of her body a half century later would suggest the side of an old building kicked in.

Rose's face in old age—the defiant eyes, Roman nose, small mouth and tightly-combed silver hair—suggested something else. For the hospital nuns had taught her that self-pity was no virtue. In fact, strangers who looked too closely at her deformity over the years usually suffered considerable embarrassment.

"What the hell are you looking at!" she'd yell. It stopped them every time.

In the later years after he retired, John Valanti drank heavily, and when he did, he fell onto a bench near the waterfront. One day as he lay in a stupor on one of those benches, a policeman prodded him with his club, demanding that he move on. The old man was defiant. The cop hit him. The old man tried to fight, and the cop hit him hard on the head, finally landing enough blows to render the old man unconscious enroute to the drunk tank. As it turned out, the beating also helped John Valanti to a state hospital for the insane.

Rose brought him sweets and home-cooked food, and she bathed him and talked with him when his delirium abated enough to permit it. He lived to be 79, a gaunt, shadowy old man, still at the state hospital when he died.

His daughter grew into a surprisingly attractive woman. Pictures from that time show her with a full figure, luxuriant dark hair and a classic Roman face. She was slightly over five feet tall, and she wore full skirts and dresses that disguised her deformity very well. Still, she was a cripple, and by thirty, she had no marriage prospects. One of her few social outlets was The Handicapped Club on Washington Street, where she met friends, played cards and occasionally gossiped about the problems of fellow club members.

She met Bill Bon Viso there during the early years of World War II. He was a regular visitor, generally found hunched over one of the card tables examining a gin rummy hand with a cool, practiced eye. He had wavy, jet black hair, and he was short, solid and as chunky as the stump of an old tree. He belonged to the club because of his artificial leg, which was attached to his thigh above the place where his knee once was and secured by canvas straps— the result of a teenage baseball spiking accident that led to infection, gangrene, and finally amputation.

Rose Valanti saw only his smile. It spread across his face then and for the next twenty-five years like a warm ray of light. His smiles seemed almost beatific—so resonant of an inner peace that his full face seemed to glow. His eyes, almost liquid, added to the aura—eyes which sought out Rose as she walked through the club's card room, favoring her bad leg.

Rose, of course, did not like to be watched. "What the heck are you looking at?" she demanded, unconsciously softening the usual "hell" in the face of that smile.

"You," he said softly. He continued to watch her. Later he asked Rose to have coffee with him.

She refused.

He followed her home, asking again. She refused. In succeeding nights, he asked again and again. Rose always refused.

"I couldn't be going out with a married man," she explained later.

Two years later, Bill Bon Viso's first wife died in childbirth, leaving him with two young daughters. Rose heard the news through friends at the club, yet in her pride she made no effort to contact him.

Then she went to a party knowing he would be there, and he approached her almost immediately.

"You know, Rose, my wife is gone," he said, his face very soft and warm in the half light of the crowded room. "I'd like to take you out now."

"You've got children. I've gotta go out with you with two kids?" She still had her pride.

"If you care for me, you'll have them, too."

They were married within the year. It was 1944, and Bill's daughters, Sandy and Sophie, had lived with relatives until then. Suddenly at 32 Rose had a husband and a family. Bill moved all of them into a four-room apartment on East Fifth Street, a third floor walkup. The rent was $37 a month, and the apartment happened to be on the same block as the Ninth Precinct headquarters where Pete, twenty-five years later, would report to work.

The child, born April 23, 1948, came into the world easily, weighing seven pounds, eight ounces. Rose was not as healthy as her son. The infirmary kept her in bed for 18 days and said she could not endure another pregnancy. She was sterilized.

Still, Rose was buoyant. She'd had trouble with her adopted daughters, who did not accept her easily. They had acquired independent ways living with indulgent kin, and they often challenged Rose's authority. Bill, on the other hand, had proved to be a near-perfect husband, a quiet, thoughtful presence in her life who provided her with the security and love she had craved so long. She desperately wanted to give him a son, and now she had.

She had an *Italian* family now, and she was proud. A photograph shows Rose happily holding the baby. She wears a crucifix and smiles widely over it. Bill Bon Viso stands next to her in a baggy suit, short and square like his tiny, fullfigured wife. The baby is draped in white, and his feet are fitted with white crocheted booties. He has fat cheeks, an odd look of displeasure on his miniature face, and a defiant lower lip. Already the startling eyes glow.

Bill never philandered in his second marriage. He played cards, gambled and went to the races, but he risked only money he saved by working overtime. After a day at Aqueduct, or a night of cards in one of the neighborhood social clubs, he often brought Rose flowers. Rose seldom knew if he had won or lost; he didn't talk about it. And she couldn't compute the rise or fall of his fortunes by the household money he gave her, because the money was always the same, whether he went to the track or not.

At the machine shop where he worked, Bill won the checkers championship and brought home a small trophy; but he tired of the job. Shortly after the Korean war he moved to the docks, where one of his brothers, a long-shoreman and a member of an organized crime family, got him on as a "checker," keeping track of things that came and went and supervising the loading of trucks. He eventually left for a similar job in the storage warehouses of W. T. Grant. The warehouses happened to be across the street from the city housing project where he had moved his family during the Fifties, and for many years he walked less than a block to work. But the company moved to New Jersey, and though Bill Bon Viso was invited to go along, he decided against commuting and found a job as a film splicer in midtown Manhattan, where he worked until he died.

Bill never really liked changing jobs. "Put your head to becoming something," he told his son. "Get a career. When I was a young man, I didn't care about anything. I went from job to job, and it's not good that way. You've got no security."

And Pete Bon Viso listened, as he did whenever his father talked.

Pete was a popular kid who seemed to sail on the clouds of childhood as if they would support him forever. In 1951,

Bill moved the family into a six-room apartment in The Smith, one of the city's newest housing projects. Pete played in the parks and playgrounds provided by the Housing Authority, explored the construction sites of the unfinished towers, and watched the boats pass on the East River. He was a friendly kid, one who got along: alert eyes, a quick smile, the good sense to let the worst trouble pass by. His one mark of early childhood was an apricot-sized scar acquired when as a toddler he'd pulled a pan of boiling water off the kitchen table and splashed it over his face, neck and shoulders. Bill Bon Viso happened to be standing nearby, and he grabbed his screaming son and dabbed milk on his scalded skin except for a spot where Pete's T-shirt stuck to him. When the T-shirt came off, the skin followed it, leaving the scar.

Another scar would develop soon. "Mom," he said to Rose one day. "Why don't you have a brother for me?"

"Honey, I'm sorry," she said, leaning down and stroking his head. "I can't for the world have a brother for you."

One of Pete's best boyhood friends, Tommy Ryan, now a bank manager with a raspy voice and a penchant for drinking himself into oblivion on weekends, had four. Pete envied him deeply. Yet he was also frightened and confused when Tommy and his brothers fought, or when Tommy's father hit Tommy, often in drunken anger. Seeing this, he became visibly upset, sometimes to the edge of tears.

Bill Bon Viso spent a great deal of time with Pete. He made his son a slingshot from a forked tree branch and tire tube; and he made himself one. On Sundays Bill and Pete sat by the river and shot marbles at unwary seagulls.

Pete soon could take a gull down at 50 yards. But it was the conversations—"just bullshitting and sitting around"— that he loved most. Sometimes Bill Bon Viso and his son seemed more like brothers.

Pete took that same slingshot one night and ventured out to see what impression he could make on the neighborhood's street lamps.

"It took me about three shots for each lamp," he remembers. "One shot for the outside glass and two to get the light. I did about eight lamps before the housing cops grabbed me by the collar and brought me up to my father."

But Bill Bon Viso, in a pattern that would hold, said nothing. He quietly told the policemen that he would "take care of this," and then gave his son the gentlest of reprimands. "Now," he said, "I've gotta make another slingshot."

Next, he taught Pete to gamble. By the age of seven, Pete could play almost any game—poker, Gin Rummy, Blackjack, Canasta—and he could shoot craps. He was a natural at cards, partly because he was good at arithmetic.

In the first grade one day, Pete's teacher wrote each letter of the alphabet on the blackboard. She then counted the 26 letters, and explained that there were both capital and small letters.

"Now, class, everyone knows there are twenty-six letters in the alphabet," she said. "How many letters would we have on the board if there were twenty-six big ones and twenty-six little ones?"

A tiny hand shot up. The young teacher, surprised at such a quick response, glanced at her seating chart.

"Yes, Pete?"

"That's fifty-two," Pete said brightly.

The woman was stunned. She'd expected that a child who figured out the answer would have to count the letters, slowly.

"How did you know?"

'There's fifty-two cards in a deck," Pete said, "and half a deck is twenty-six. So if there's two times twenty-six, it's gotta be fifty-two. That's how I know."

Pete's teacher was quiet for a moment. "That's right," she said, ending the lesson.

By his eighth birthday, Pete knew every card game Bill could teach him. He'd also developed a taste for the excitement that money added to these games. On holidays, relatives often dropped by the Bon Viso house to play nickel-and-dime poker. Pete sat in, bringing about two dollars to the table from a special shoe box.

One holiday, Pete leaned toward his father and whispered loudly: "Does five of the same suit make a flush?"

Bill Bon Viso beamed. He knew that Pete knew the answer, but he said yes in an equally loud stage whisper and folded his own hand.

Pete's bluff won the pot. Rose objected. Hustling will cause him trouble when he's older, she protested. But her husband disagreed. If he knows these tricks now, he won't be fooled later, Bill insisted.

On Fridays, father and son joined the Handicapped Club's weekly gin rummy game. They went other nights to a neighborhood social club for poker. The games involved only nickels and dimes, but Pete was thrilled to be at an illegal game in a secret back room. Even then, he was hooked.

They played other games. Bill Bon Viso had modest hopes that his son would become a baseball player, and he was a patient, careful coach. He showed Pete everything he knew about the game, and he wasn't a bad player himself. Bill moved quickly, hit well and had a strong right arm; it was hard to tell, in fact, that one of his legs was made of wood (and later plastic). Most of the neighborhood remained unaware of this handicap until his death. He covered it so well that Pete preferred that his father, rather than Rose, come to school if there was trouble. Rose walked with an obvious, almost lurching limp, and she embarrassed him furher by punishing him publicly.

Bill had a way of walking that covered all but the tiniest trace of his trouble, and he remained cool. And clearly, as Pete later came to know—as he would know few things so well in his life—it mattered to Bill a great deal that the world see nothing unusual about the Bon Viso family.

Whatever Pete really felt about his parents' deformities usually stayed below the surface of his happy-go-lucky smile. But not entirely. Tommy Ryan complained of his father's drinking one day, almost in tears.

"You should be grateful," Pete cut in suddenly. "At least there's nothing *wrong* with your dad."

"You kidding?" Tommy shot back. "Your father plays baseball with you! Mine never comes out! He just sits home and drinks!" Tommy caught his breath. "Nobody can tell your dad has a bad leg unless they look close."

And Pete lowered his eyes and thought about this. Somewhere in a place where his anger and fear came together, he still envied Tommy for having parents who looked like everyone else.

Rose worked throughout Pete's childhood, leaving the day-to-day duty of feeding Pete, combing his hair and sending him to school to his sister, Sandy, who by then was a teenager. Rose's absence sometimes upset the young boy, but he eventually realized that she was gone each morning because the family needed the money she earned. In fact, his mother's years of work left a deep impression on him, one that would ultimately put a great distance between Pete and the people he policed.

"My parents were *both* handicapped," he'd say again and again, choking angrily as the words come out. "They were never on welfare. It pisses me off *a lot* to see healthy people out there getting free money. My mother was a cleaning woman all her life, and she still is. She would clean somebody else's house to buy me another pair of shoes. That's what my mother did all my life. I see a lotta *healthy* people on welfare, you know?"

In elementary school one day early in the term, the teacher asked each member of her class to give his or her name, date of birth, and nationality. Pete was the eighth student to do this; before him, kids with Polish and Jewish names identified themselves as "American."

"My name is Peter Bon Viso," he said brightly. "I was born April 23rd, 1948. I'm Italian."

The woman slammed her blackboard eraser down with a thudding cloud of dust and looked at Pete.

"I knew it," she said. "Every student I have who is Italian-American says he is Italian, not Italian-American or just plain American. Why?"

"I don't know," the little boy answered timidly.

"I still don't know," Pete said twenty years later. "I didn't speak Italian at all, and I wasn't born in Italy. My mother was born in this country; so was my father. Maybe I thought I was Italian because I ate spaghetti every Sunday and every Thursday I ate it again."

With all this, Pete and his friends considered themselves true native sons. They were tough little daredevils, prowling the streets in search of prankish adventure. They drank beer in dark hallways as their fathers did before them, and they planned to step grandly into the American dream. They would carry on the ethnic and religious traditions where it was convenient. Where it was not, they would change things.

Pete was 11 when he entered his Robin Hood phase.

He saw himself as a member of the "underclass," and the idea served him well. He lived in a housing project in a ghetto neighborhood, and so stealing was not, well, not exactly, a crime. True, he was not a member of a broken, alcoholic or heroin debased family. He had food on his table at night, shelter, security. Yet the *ambiance* of his life was poverty. Many of his friends in the projects came from ravaged families. They stole; and so it followed that Pete did, too.

Besides, Bill and Rose couldn't afford the things he wanted.

"If I needed some baseball equipment, I'd get my duffel bag and go down to Martino's or Davega's. I'd pick up some baseball socks or steal myself another glove, and it was no big deal. We did it practically every other week.

"I was fucking around with a 15 pound dumbbell at

Herman's on Nassau Street on Saturday when no sales people were around. I just put it in the duffel bag and walked out."

Pete shrugged. He was wearing a brown patterned knit shirt, opened half way down his chest showing dark curly hair and a gold St. Christopher's medal dangling on a thin gold chain, the day he talked about this. "I didn't think I was doing anything that bad. I never hurt anybody, and I was a needy kid besides. I couldn't have done violence, and I never took money from poor people."

Pete's scores had to have style. He took a leather jacket out of Modell's one day, thinking it was one of the biggest scores in his life. It didn't fit him, but he put it on and walked out.

"It was about nine sizes too big for me, but it seemed terrific that I got it. Like people would say: hey, that Pete's got some pair of balls. Hey, that kid Bon Viso is *crazy.*"

Crazy? He liked the idea. It meant brave, reckless, something apart. He liked that, and he liked the attention it brought him.

He pushed his luck relentlessly. He and Tommy Ryan lifted weights at home several times a week, and on Saturdays, they walked across the Manhattan bridge to use the weight room at the St. George Hotel in Brooklyn Heights. And one night they threw a bowling ball off the bridge to see what sort of splash it would make, narrowly missing a tugboat.

Another night, they broke into the State Motor Vehicles Building through a side window—and barely escaped when an alarm went off. Whenever a building was abandoned in the neighborhood, they broke into it and stole whatever they could find, breaking the windows and claiming the space as their own until the wrecking crews arrived.

For spare change, they sometimes took the heads off parking meters. At an impromptu neighborhood party, angry when some girls ignored them, they ransacked the apartment, stealing wristwatches, clothing, a jar of pennies and the owner's pornography collection.

Ironically, without knowing it, Pete was training himself for police work. He'd already acquired a street sense few cops could match. But now he was going an extra mile for the City of New York, learning to *think* like a criminal. In the end, there would be few cops in the Ninth as instinctively in touch with the criminal mind. Something in the felon's eyes, or the way he held himself, transmitted a familiar signal to Pete. He would use the knowledge on Avenue C.

Car theft and burglary remained. In Pete's neighborhood, joy riding was nearly as well organized as Little League.

"We had one car, an old '55 Chevy, that we took out whenever we wanted it. We used it so often that we liked to put it in the same parking spot afterward so as not to make the people nervous. After a while we started leaving them notes like, 'We filled the tank.' It got like a game. The people started parking the car farther and farther from their building, but we'd always find it and take it out and try to put it back in the same spot. If we couldn't, we'd leave a note on the next car saying where it was. It got to the point where the guy fucked up the radio to discourage us, but we took the car anyway. Sometimes we'd leave him five dollars, and we always tried to replace the gas."

Pete looked down at his hands and smiled.

"Sometimes we left a few beer cans around, which we shoulda straightened out. We tried to take good care of the car because we figured this was something we could have steady. I guess the guy finally couldn't take the pressure. One day it was just gone. We figured he sold it—or drove it off a cliff. We never did find out who he was."

But it was good police training.

"After taking a few joy rides, you start accumulating keys." Pete's face assumed a serious expression. "Back then, General Motors keys were common; they fit almost any General Motors car. So I had a bunch of keys I used pretty regularly. When I became a cop, I used them again. If Paul and I found an abandoned or stolen car that wasn't stripped yet, we could start it up and drive it down to the station house so the department could notify the owner, you know?"

At 15, Pete started a lucrative sideline in counterfeit Selective Service cards. He bought them in lots of 50 for two dollars each from a girl at his high school whose boy friend was a printer, and sold them for five. They got you into bars. In grade school, he had sold phony baptismal certificates, which got you into pool halls.

A side benefit of such enterprise was that Pete himself could get into bars. He was at a bar on Worth Street one night with Tommy Ryan, who was 17, and another friend named Robbie, 16, who is now in prison on the West

Coast. The bar served beer in large tumblers for a quarter; it seemed to Pete the best quarter he'd ever spent. He spent another, and another after that, and pretty soon he and Tommy and Robbie began making plans. They decided to try something a little different and left Fellini's and walked down Park Row.

They saw a pawn shop and decided to burglarize it. The three drunken teen-agers stood in front of the shop's window and discussed technique. Pete thought it would be great to steal some guns. They decided to climb the next door building's fire escape, jump across to the roof and break in through the skylight. They were flying; they had no idea what they were risking. They climbed drunkenly to the roof and crossed over; and then, seeing a skylight, leaned over the building's edge and checked to make sure they saw the three balls below them.

Kicking open the skylight, they found a small metal ladder leading into the building's darkness. They climbed inside and lit matches and discovered they were in the storage room of a novelty shop. They found no guns, just crates of stuffed animals, party hats and wooden spears with rubber tips. They climbed down another floor.

More stuffed animals, party hats and wooden spears.

More of the same on the ground floor. Instead of guns, they would settle for toys. They were not a team to lose heart easily. They started carrying boxes of animals and hats up the metal ladder to the roof.

Pete heard a noise as he carried a box of toys to the fire escape, and he looked over the edge of the building and saw half a dozen radio cars. Cops were running in all directions.

They threw the loot down the skylight, closed it and ran to the fire escape. A wave of giggles washed over them as they clambered down the metal ladder. It all seemed very funny.

But a cop stood below them aiming his service revolver up the ladder.

"Hands on your head!"

Suddenly the three ace cat burglars were drunken teen-age clowns trying to climb down a steep ladder without holding the hand railing. Eventually they stood uneasily on the ground and submitted to a search. In a hurried, whispered conference they decided to say they were playing Ringelevio and hide-and-seek. Arriving at the Fifth precinct, Tommy and Robbie were taken into separate rooms by detectives. Pete, classified as a juvenile offender, sat in the squad room unmolested.

"What were you doing?" he heard a detective ask Robbie.

"We wuz playin'!"

Pete was sitting between stereo speakers, for now he heard the other detective ask Tommy: "What were you doing on the roof?"

"We wuz playin'!"

Each detective asked each teen-ager the same question again; and again. Pete cocked his head toward Robbie's room in one direction, then toward the squad room lockers where Tommy was held. As the questions continued, threats came.

"You kids are fulla shit! I'm askin' you one more time, and I'm gonna smack youse in the mouth."

From the other room: "You're fulla shit, goddamit! I'm

askin' you one more time, and I'm gonna kick youse in the
balls, you understand?"

Pete's eyes widened.

"What were you doing on the roof?"

"What were you doing on the fuckin' roof?"

"We wuz playin'."

"We wuz playin' Ringelevio."

Whap! Robbie began to cry. Whoomp! Tommy's chair
crashed to the floor. And Pete, safe from anything more
than a juvenile court reprimand that wouldn't go into his
permanent record, began to laugh to hard that he nearly
lost his balance. Tommy was dragged out of the locker
room area holding himself between the legs; Robbie came
out crying. The detectives, angry but unable to do anything
more, called the store owner who decided not to press
charges.

As usual, Bill Bon Viso had very little to say. "My father
never did anything," Pete shrugged. "He said it was a stupid
thing to do, and what the fuck was I out drinking for anyway? I coulda fallen off the roof. I coulda got hurt."

Rose Bon Viso had a different approach. She became
very excited and hit her son several times. It was hard for
her to reach him because she was so short, so she waited
until Pete was sitting down—and suddenly slapped him.
She had begun to do it often as her son's troubles escalated.
Sometimes she did it in front of his friends. He could not
protest; it was not the Italian way. So he laughed, pretend-
ing it didn't hurt. That angered Rose further, and she usually reached for a shoe. This stopped him, since he knew
she would use it, following him to bed if necessary.

In those moments, Bill Bon Viso never raised his voice. If he had something to say, he'd say it privately. His anger surfaced only once during those years. Pete had gotten into a bad fight at high school and had been suspended. His parents were deeply upset. The following morning, Bill sat at the kitchen table eating cereal and milk as Pete walked by.

Rose trapped him at the door. "You gonna tell your father what happened?" she demanded.

"I ain't gonna tell him nothin'."

Suddenly Pete was covered with cereal and milk. He had shown no respect, and Bill had thrown the cereal bowl at him. Half an hour later, Pete approached his father to apologize. Bill said he was sorry, too.

Yet in a strange way, Bill and Rose Bon Viso disciplined their son very well. For Pete's sixteenth birthday, the magic age separating New York City children from adult offenders, arrived as an absolution. He went "straight." His life abruptly calmed down as if a storm had blown itself out, however improbable it may have seemed to his friends at the time. Somehow he knew that his life had to change. It was possible to be interrogated by detectives who might hurt you now. It was suddenly possible to go to jail, or at least a junior form of it. And it was possible to have a criminal record. And so Pete Bon Viso, a pragmatist, a kid who thought so often about his future, suddenly, strangely, became a model citizen. He considered a career; he settled down with a steady girlfriend. He started thinking about becoming a policeman.

CHAPTER 4

BEHIND the counter of his Avenue C cleaning establishment, Abie Schwartz played the odds carefully: he carried a gun. It was duly registered, and Abie, a nervous little man with bony hands and Bugs Bunny teeth, had the skill and temperament to use it. As a teen-ager in Vienna, the only child of a Jewish textile sorter, he ran messages for the Underground—until the Gestapo kicked in his door one night and eventually put him on a train to Dachau. He spent six years there, starving, constantly thinking about the gas.

"You weren't sure of your life anytime," he remembers. "So what could scare me on Avenue C?" His voice rises and he throws up his bony hands. "I don't *know* fear!" Abie has a serious ulcer condition, thanks to his nervous temperament and six years of substandard prison camp rations. When angry, he turns nearly purple.

And an argument involving the Jewish question will change his already high voice into a siren the equal of any police car. A black man walked into Abie's cleaners shortly after he had set up shop and called him a "Jew bastard." Abie knocked him to the floor with a baseball bat; he screamed and kicked the man repeatedly and continued to scream as he threw him out. Word got around he was not to be bothered, ever.

Abie is hardly imposing. At best, he weighs 105 pounds after a good meal, and he stands five feet two inches tall, not even fly weight class. Yet he has a sense of cause about him and the obvious willingness to fight for his beliefs. He was tortured repeatedly in Dachau, but kept tight company with other defiant Jews and survived. After the war, he made his way to New York to join his family, which had emigrated after his capture, and found a job in a leather factory; later, he drove a taxi. In 1957, he found work in a dry cleaning shop on the Lower East Side. Eventually he became the shop's manager.

Avenue C for decades had been home to a settled-in population of Ukrainians and Eastern European Jews. But by 1963, when Abie bought a marginal dry cleaning store near the corner of Ninth Street (it cost $1000 and he put $8000 into a new boiler and a pressing machine), the area's ethnic makeup had changed startlingly to a majority of Puerto Ricans and blacks. Abie and other white merchants had hoped that the rise of city-sponsored middle-income apartments near Fourteenth Street would bring money into the neighborhood, but they were sadly wrong.

The urban renewal scheduled to accompany the apartments became bogged down in city funding disputes; the neighborhood fell fast to poverty and heroin. Abie began to notice junkies nodding out on the parking meters outside his store. He heard stories of thieves and addicts burning down buildings on side streets so they could scavenge and sell the metal plumbing and electrical fixtures. The majority of families near his store lived on welfare; they bought groceries on credit at the bodegas (which survived by giving it) and paid when the checks arrived. The pharmacy next to Abie stayed open because of Medicaid receipts. And soon Abie had trouble staying afloat. He began taking money orders ("Giro's"), and he inaugurated three hour service.

After that, ghetto politics added to his troubles. He learned that his store had been selected for trashing during the period of unrest following Martin Luther King's death. Already shops to the south of him had been looted.

"Abie, tonight the rest of the stores are gonna go," a friend named Angelo warned him. "It's nothing against you personally. It's just gonna happen." At the time, Mayor John Lindsay had ordered his Tactical Patrol Forces to withdraw from the area in hopes of cooling things down. Abie immediately called the Jewish Defense League. He asked for men with guns, and a number of people agreed to come. Then he marched furiously into the Ninth Precinct.

"If you think for one minute I'm standing by and let them destroy the store I worked twelve years for like a mule while a cop with a gun and helmet stands by and does nothing," he screamed at the startled precinct commander, "you're crazy! I say, *fuck* Lindsay and his policies —he don't put a *dime* in my pocket! If you don't want no corpses on the street tonight, you better do something. The JDL is moving in!"

As a result, the Tactical Patrol Force secured Avenue C above Eighth Street, and Abie's store survived.

Still, when Pete began working the avenue in 1971, Abie was making little or no money. His wholesale shirt receipts had dropped from eighty to fifteen dollars a week in the course of a year. And his Puerto Rican wife (he had met her in the store) had divorced him and gone back to the island. The Spanish businesses on nearby blocks were surviving by taking numbers.

"The store wasn't much more than a place to hang out," he remembers, smiling sadly. "And terrible frightening things were happening. I saw junkies everywhere. They sold heroin all over—across the street, by my front door. The junkies nodded outside my window, falling all over the place, young kids and everything."

Abie's spirit stayed strong. He kept an open bottle of Scotch in the shop and always offered drinks to friends who dropped in, including Pete and Paul. He bet regularly with a Jewish bookie down the block; and a number of neighborhood characters congregated regularly in the shop, providing him with company and protection from random street harrassments.

He still had his temper.

An imposing black man, easily six feet tall, walked into the shop one day and threw his ticket contemptuously in Abie's face.

"Gimme my motherfuckin' pants, man," he said.

"There's the motherfuckin' door! Get the fuck out!"

Abie screamed. "You talk to me like a *man* if you want
your pants."

The tall man laughed and apologized, and he and Abie
were friends thereafter.

It happened that Victorio Sanchez also brought his
clothes to Abie. Abie remembers him as a muscular little
man who paid his tickets with crumpled bills pulled out
of a side pocket. Abie knew nothing about him, largely because Sanchez offered no more than a sullen mask during
these encounters. He met Abie's eyes across the counter
with a glassy stare; that was all.

By the time their lives brushed so rudely against Sanchez,
Pete and Paul seemed almost oblivious to the outside world.
They seemed obsessed with each other. They ate, drank
and prowled the city together, seeing each other more than
they saw their wives. They slept at Rose's apartment
several nights a week, and Paul called her "Mom." It was
one of the happiest times of Pete's life. He called Paul his
brother. They rode to work together, they spent their working days with each other. When they were drinking and
telling stories, they seemed to have traveled to a world of
their own making. They were high on each other—lovers
in every way but sexually.

Five days a week, they walked Avenue C, given responsibility for the avenue and half a block of each of its side
streets. The side streets, filled with decaying tenements
and downtrodden businesses, joined Avenue C like ribs
attached to a diseased backbone. The avenue itself was lined
with stores like Los Muchachos Bodega, Freddie's Lunch-

eonette, Little Luis' Wholesale Eggs, Cuchifritos stands, beauty parlors, furniture and junk stores, fruit stands, "bargain" stores, dark bars filled with daytime drinkers, and private gin rummy and pool parlors like the "Avenue C Club," which was located behind a battered and unmarked green door midway down the avenue.

The overall effect was something like seeing San Juan, Tel Aviv, and Dodge City mixed together. The cowboys were black and Puerto Rican, the townspeople Jewish. Pete and Paul, playing deputy sheriffs, walked the crowded avenue each day among restless gangs of black and Hispanic youths, numbers runners, junkies and winos. The avenue was dirty and desperate; it fascinated the young cops.

The day's rounds usually began at a candy and news counter near 13th Street. It was owned by a short, chubby Jewish man who had two partners, and it was little more than a large, street-level hole in the building, its coffee urn and candy bars behind the cash register, piles of newspapers against the opposite wall. The man was always glad to see them, since their visits lessened his likelihood of trouble that day. He also fed Pete and Paul the latest neighborhood intelligence, as did countless others on the avenue whose lot was improved rather than threatened by an active cop team. Pete did the talking while Paul read the papers. Pete was the talker; Paul, the silent one.

They moved to the corner of 10th Street next, an area plagued regularly by purse snatchers. Gabays, an odd-lot warehouse dealing in everything from furniture to argyle socks, was nearby; and Tommy's Cadillac, its chauffeur waiting, was often parked outside. Tommy, past his prime now, had controlled a number of speakeasies in the thirties, and he seemed to have made it out to pasture safely—at least as evidenced by the Cadillac, the dark cashmere coat, broad-brimmed fedora, Italian shoes and dollar cigar sticking out of his mouth like the precinct house flagpole.

He liked to talk about his old speakeasies.

"It cost me $60,000 to fix up that room," he would say to anyone foolish enough to ask about the Good Old Days. "I called my people—I had good people—and I said get these Guinea bastards off my back." He pulled on the stovepipe-sized cigar, blowing out a thick cloud of smoke. "I'm Italian myself, you know? But these bastards were messing things up. They weren't trying to take me over, but they were hopping from table to table, bothering my customers and all. I didn't need that kind of business, I didn't need it at all. So I got things straightened out . . ."

"Hey, Tommy, we gotta see some people," Pete would say, leaving the old man to his memories, or fantasies. "We'll be back, okay?"

On a morning tour, they'd wave to Smilin' Jack, who ran a fruit stand across from Abie's. Jack came out before the rest of the avenue, traveling before dawn to Hunt's Point Market in the Bronx and back with his fruit. After a visit to the pharmacist at the corner of Tenth Street, they generally dropped into Abie's. It might be 8:15 A.M., but the bottle was ready. In the mornings, they generally refused.

Not all cops did. Abie remembers a sanitation department cop who waited each morning at eight for him to open the store. Most days, of course, Abie drank with him.

"In some ways, Pete and Paul were fuckups, and a lot of people knew it," Abie remembers. "But they were good cops, and they were liked in the community. They never went after anybody who didn't deserve it. And they *never* expected favors. We drank together, but they paid as often as I did. We had sausage and beer. Sometimes I paid, sometimes they paid. They always paid their share. They even watched the store sometimes while I went out to get a sandwich or something."

Before the city-sponsored hearings on police corruption in 1970, Abie took a fair amount of abuse from cops on his beat. They expected handouts at the holidays, and it was understood that he would clean their uniforms for free. But after that year, the system changed; and Pete and Paul and the other neighborhood police teams were part of the new order, leaning in the other direction if anything. Abie took their sports action to *his* bookie, for example.

Sam's Wholesale Candy Shop, near Sixth Street, air-conditioned in the summer, was a mandatory stop. The old man, portly and bald, seemed glad to see them. He wore a cap indoors and kept a pencil behind his ear, and he talked of the old days on the Avenue, when it was safe, he insisted, to sleep on the fire escape at night. He'd been around 40 years.

Sam's shop was a peanut and chocolate wonderland. Pete, who dieted regularly, considered the shop a major challenge. Could he stop at one chocolate? Paul preferred Sam's peanuts. He also liked the attention he got when he popped a whole one into his mouth, chomping down on the shell with a loud crackle.

By 10:30, they usually reached Fourth Street, their territory's southern border. A numbers man in a green felt hat might be standing outside of Freddie's Luncheonette taking one and two dollar bets: nothing unusual. A walk down nearby Fifth Street, past the garage dealing in stolen auto parts, past abandoned buildings that looked out at the street with blank window-eyes, usually forced Pete to break up several crap games.

"Do it inside," he'd say, throwing his head back slightly. "You play out here, you make me look bad, right?" His understanding of the neighborhood's sociology made him enormously popular. He gave no parking tickets, preferring to go into the nearby shops and find the car's owner.

And the neighborhood knew that Pete patronized the man in the green felt hat as much as anyone.

In the larger sense, Pete knew instinctively that he couldn't change anything. It would take an army to stop all the petty crime on the avenue—and for what? Gambling and drugs, however destructive, were part of peoples' lives here. Take them away, and give nothing back, and you've robbed them of what little romance their dreary lives held. You might as well stop them from drinking and making love. Pete's job was simply to keep things reasonably quiet —at least until the next generation of poor people came in with *its* set of rules.

In the meantime, he bought a cheap Afro wig at Gabay's one day and took it into a beauty parlor near Seventh Street to be brushed out. And then he wore it all day, flattened slightly by his patrolman's hat, enjoying the smiles and double-takes it brought. He also took to wearing blue sneakers, reasoning he could chase criminals better—and more comfortably.

July 22, 1972: Five days after the bread-truck arrest, they

returned to the avenue. Word of the incident had spread. A lieutenant, the day's patrol supervisor, drove up and chatted amiably for a few minutes. Storekeepers up and down the line offered compliments; and as the afternoon wore on, they dropped in on Abie.

"Hey, Pete! Hey, Paul!" he screeched happily. "Have a little scotch!"

"Abie, you gotta be kidding," Pete laughed. "It's ninety degrees out there. How can you drink scotch on a day like this?"

"So you wanta beer? Lemme get you a beer."

"You talked us into it."

The usual crowd was hanging around. Abie pulled a crumpled bill out of his pocket and sent one of the hangers-on across the street for a six-pack. He was back with the beer quickly, and everyone relaxed for a moment.

And someone outside screamed in Spanish, splitting the hot July air.

Pete and Paul dropped the beer, threw on their hats and rushed out of the shop. The air was still now, and whoever had screamed was gone. Pete focused on a short dark man standing on the corner of Tenth Street. He was a startling sight: squat and burr-headed with a sweating, angry face. His clothing was completely black as if he was foreign and apart from his surroundings. He walked slowly toward Pete and Paul without seeming to see them. As he walked, three people, two men and a woman, joined him and walked with him.

"Paul, he's got a gun!" Pete warned his partner.

Pete had seen a frighteningly large pistol. It had a six-inch barrel, and like everything else about the man, it was black, cradled in the man's hand and hidden against the darkness of his clothing.

Pete reached for his service revolver. It was his habit to first break his holster's safety catch, pausing before actually drawing the gun, but today he was frightened enough to raise the pistol immediately. Paul had tried to draw his revolver, too; but the gun had become entangled with his nightstick strap, and he couldn't free it as they hurried toward the gunman.

Victorio Sanchez, known in the neighborhood as "Blackie," hadn't seen the cops. He put the massive pistol in his waistband and kept walking. Right now he was high. Things were blurry, for in the thirty-third year of his troubled life, he was shooting four bags of heroin a day; and that day, if witnesses were to be believed, he'd used the big gun in at least two armed robberies. He'd also fired it repeatedly at an addict-dealer on Tenth Street after accusing him half an hour earlier of selling contaminated heroin.

Pete Bon Viso and he were 20 feet apart now, standing in front of Marvin's, a decaying bar next to Abie's. Still unaware of the two young cops, Sanchez turned toward his friends. Pete and Paul stopped now, and Pete raised his service revolver to the level of Sanchez's chest, planting his feet slightly apart on the pavement, holding the gun with two hands.

"Hands up! Police!"

Sanchez saw his antagonists. And he reached for the dark gun in his waistband.

The law at this moment permitted Pete Bon Viso to kill him. Sanchez had the long-barreled .38 in his hand, and he was bringing it up. In less than half a second, Pete could easily have fired his service revolver, which was aimed at the gunman's heart.

Pete's memory reared like a frightened stallion. In the heartbeat that he held the gun on Sanchez, he remembered speeding to East 11th Street a year earlier, where a man with a gun was said to be threatening his neighbors. Pete had found the man, clearly drunk, standing beside a parked car and holding a gun in another man's stomach, and Pete had raised his own gun, cocked it, and ordered the man to drop his. The man had turned and looked into the barrel of Pete's .38 and for a moment had had trouble making sense of his situation. Then he'd lifted his hands, as if to surrender—but with his gun pointed directly at Pete.

"I figured he was trying to take me out," Pete recalled later. "As I was squeezing off the shot, which takes about half a second or a little longer because you squeeze slowly and you never really know when it's gonna go off, he dropped the gun. It hit the ground. I heard it hit, and the pressure went off my trigger finger immediately. I felt a sigh of relief. I would have killed him in half a second."

It was that simple. A jabbering, drunken man with blood and oxygen running through him would revert to dead flesh on East 11th Street.

Pete had holstered his gun and pushed the man against the car. He had reached for the gun in the gutter and found a mockery of a gun, a carbon dioxide cartridge pistol.

"A very strange feeling came over me. I could have taken a life. I could have blown off the back of this guy's head. Legally I would have been justified. But it would have had a very strange effect on *my* life. The man had a simulated gun that couldn't hurt me, and I would have killed him for it. It was a fuckin' toy, and I almost took someone out for a toy."

The cartridge pistol, too, had had an exceptionally long barrel. . . .

"Drop that gun!" Pete yelled now at Sanchez.

By the book, Pete should have cocked his revolver. But he just held it on Sanchez and repeated his command. Paul still hadn't untangled his gun. "If he was Annie Oakley or somebody," Pete remembers, "he could have taken us both out." Pete felt very alone.

With a swift jerky motion, Sanchez threw the gun into the Avenue's gutter.

They rushed forward. Pete handcuffed Sanchez, and Paul put his cuffs on another man who had a machete in a paper bag. Pete looked up.

"Paul, where's the gun?"

Paul saw the woman, Nilda Severo, reach down to the street and stuff the pistol into her waistband; she started to walk away.

"Pete, she's got the gun!" Without it, they had no arrest. They knew nothing of Sanchez's movements earlier that day. They'd have to let him go.

Pete had handcuffed Sanchez behind his back and now he pulled the gunman backward towards Paul, taking hold of Paul's prisoner. Paul ran and reached the girl in half a dozen galloping strides. He caught her shoulders and spun her around, reaching with his other hand for the gun.

A crowd was gathering. Pete and Paul had Sanchez, the woman and the other man, whose name was Ramos, together. But they had no handcuffs for the woman, and she shook free of Paul's grasp and started to walk away again.

As she did, Pete grabbed her roughly and pushed her back with the other prisoners.

"Hey, motherfucker," a man yelled, bursting out of the crowd and grabbing Pete, "don't push my wife!" Pete turned and hit the stranger full in the face, knocking him hard to the sidewalk, realizing suddenly that he'd seen him walking alongside Sanchez.

The crowd became noisy. Pete and Paul felt the pressure of too many people around them and became frightened, and now Paul jumped on the man on the pavement and hit him with his nightstick—again and again as the man screamed and rolled away trying to escape the falling club.

And the woman came at Paul, flailing, trying to jump on his back and pull him off. The crowd was moving about now. A street hustler picked up a rock and announced he was going to throw it at Pete. Abie Schwartz, brandishing his pistol, screamed and stopped him. Across the avenue Jack the fruit vendor watched the confrontation and called the Ninth Precinct.

A sector car arrived. Pete had hold of Sanchez and the woman and the other man, and he called out to Paul as he saw the green and white car moving toward them like a battleship, red lights flashing. Another car followed in its wake, and Pete struggled toward them, barely afloat in the crosscurrents around him, holding his prisoners desperately. They stuffed Sanchez and the others into cars and rode to the precinct house in heavy-breathing, exhausted silence.

CHAPTER 5

IN the precinct house, all was confusion and anger. The lieutenant in charge of patrol wanted the arrest's details. Pete and Paul had put him off, and he was upset.

"I asked you what you had out there!" he shouted as they came in.

"Give us a break, lieutenant," Pete pleaded. "We just went through a big thing. We'll tell you as soon as *we* know."

They herded the sullen prisoners upstairs and pushed Sanchez and the other men into the squadroom's wire-mesh cage. The man Paul had beaten limped badly and moaned and cursed as they put him inside. They handcuffed Nilda Severo to a chair, and when she was in place, they began examining the gun. Three of its shells were freshly spent, still smelling of it. But without a witness to tell them what had happened, they had no way of connecting the bullets to a crime. So far, they had only a limited case: an illegal gun, resisting arrest.

Then a short flabby black man who looked like he'd been hit by lightning burst into the squad room. He was cut and covered with bruises; his clothes were filthy and torn, his pockets had been slashed. He stormed over to the cage and started screaming at Sanchez.

"You motherfucker! You bastard!" He wheeled around like a lumpy dervish and faced Pete and Paul. "This sonofabitch tried to *kill* me! He tried to . . ."

"Whoa! Whoa! Sit down, what happened?" Pete had jumped fully out of his chair. "Tell us everything!"

The man turned out to be Ronald Benson, a neighborhood small-change hustler and drug dealer. Jumping about like a wounded grasshopper, he described rapid-fire how Sanchez and his friends had attacked him on Tenth Street, knocked him down, cut his pockets, beaten him and taken his money. And when he tried to run, they shot at him.

Pete and Paul looked at Benson as if someone had just handed them a big chocolate cake. The story explained the spent shells in Sanchez's gun. And no one could doubt that Benson, a downcast pathetic little man in his early thirties, had taken a beating.

"I was goin' shopping. I got a wife and a kid at home— we got no food in the house," Benson wailed, still hopping around. "What am I gonna do? They got my last thirty-five dollars!"

Pete asked for the bills' denominations. Three bills, said Benson, a ten, a twenty and a five. No policewoman was available to search the woman, but a search of the others had produced a ten, a five and some singles which had been vouchered as evidence.

Benson stood in front of Pete and pleaded desperately for his money. Pete held fast, insisting it was needed as "evidence." Benson protested loudly that his kids were hungry.

"Look, Ronnie, I'll loan you five dollars," Pete finally blurted out in exasperation, "but when can you get it back to me?" The hustler promised to return it in the morning when he signed a complaint in court. And he hurried off.

Another, thinner man now walked hesitantly into the squad room. Seeing Sanchez in the cage, he raised his hands to his face and began to cry quietly. He'd been robbed and badly frightened, he whimpered. Pete and Paul hustled him downstairs before he could say anything else. Benson had directly accused Sanchez and the others, and thus was lost as a lineup witness. But here, miraculously, was another one.

Luis Navarro was a frail, frightened little man who supported a wife and nine children by driving a nonunion truck. A day earlier, a woman in a doorway on Tenth Street had suggestively asked him for a match. He'd walked over to her, lit her cigarette—and found himself surrounded.

Sanchez and the others had forced him at knife point to climb four flights of tenement stairs. They had taken him into a dark apartment where he saw an old Spanish woman tied to a chair, naked, crying helplessly. They stripped him, and forced him to walk in front of them into another room, where they tied him to a chair like the woman. Then they turned the apartment upside down, threatening the woman with torture and death as they demanded money. And finally they left, taking whatever they found.

Eventually, Navarro worked free of his bonds, untied the old woman and left. He was deeply frightened; he had no thought to report the crime. He was so rattled that later on he could not remember which building he had been taken into. As a result, Pete and Paul never found the old woman, though they searched for days.

Navarro had found the courage to report the crime against him only when he heard that Sanchez was in custody. He was still frightened that friends of Sanchez would find him and hurt him. But he waited while Pete arranged a lineup. He identified his tormentors, filled out the appropriate forms, and went home.

Now, Pete got out the roller, the paper and ink pad to begin the fingerprinting. As always, the process required the cooperation of the individual attached to the fingers, and sometimes an accused criminal might lose his head and become upset about the whole thing. Sanchez was first today. Pete was resolved to be patient.

The gunman gave him no help. He wiggled his fingers at the wrong moment; or he put the wrong finger in the wrong space. Sometimes he refused to cooperate at all, holding his hands woodenly at his sides.

Fairly soon, Pete had ruined several cards.

"Hold still, wouldja?"

"Fuck you, man."

Paul pulled out his sap, rose quietly, and walked over to them. He slapped Sanchez *hard* across the backs of his bare thighs.

The squat man jumped high—and then he lunged for Paul. But as he turned, Pete hit him at the base of his skull, and he fell heavily to the floor, where Pete and Paul kicked him repeatedly, then lifted him up and threw him back in the cage.

The other prisoners took the fingerprinting exercises calmly, chastened by the example.

It was time for another round. Sanchez charged, head down, like a bull. He shoved Pete aside and stomped angrily after Paul. It was an irrational act. He had been arrested before: he had to know that cops in a stationhouse would not take this.

Pete grabbed him roughly from behind and threw him into the wall. Sanchez stood dumbly against it, stunned from the impact. Then Paul came at him with the leather sap. Sanchez struck out, kicking and punching—another mistake. Pete was on him now. The two cops went after him, and he went down, scrambling away from them on his hands and knees.

While other patrolmen and detectives loitered about, filled out forms and went about their business, Pete and Paul kicked and punched the crawling Sanchez like a bloody soccer ball. The gunman groveled on the floor and began to cry. He was taking blows on the head, in the ribs, between his legs, on the shoulders and back. He cried out loudly, begging them to stop.

"Okay, Vic," Pete said, picking him up like a sack of potatoes, "you're gonna hafta go through with it, right?" Pete slapped the whimpering Sanchez on the cheeks a few times in a half-friendly way. "No sense fuckin' around," he concluded. "Let's just get it over with."

Sanchez nodded.

But when Pete tried another fingerprint card, Sanchez pulled back his hand, again. Pete's face flashed furiously red. In a flurry of fists, he pummeled Sanchez to the floor again, screaming and cursing. Paul jumped in ferociously, bringing the sap down again and again like a plantation whip. Like a wounded crab, Sanchez tried to scuttle away from them on his hands and knees. They fell on him, kicking and punching. He crawled under a table. They threw it aside, grabbing his legs and dragging him out.

As he kicked and screamed, they hoisted him up to their shoulders and carried him pell-mell toward an open window. They were on the second floor of the building.

Sanchez screamed loudly and fought hard, stiffening his body so they couldn't lift him over the sill. Squirming and kicking, he reached desperately for a steam pipe and closed his fingers around it, screaming as Paul pounded on his fingers with the sap. For a moment it truly seemed that Pete and Paul were about to throw the squat, tough, defiant hoodlum out of the second story window like a bag of garbage.

"I'm sorry, I'm sorry!" he screamed. "Please, I'm sorry!" And, smiling darkly, they let him down. He was convinced. He submitted to the fingerprinting.

One detail, medical care, remained. The impulsive husband who had belatedly rushed into the Avenue C melee was discovered to have a fractured ankle. Sanchez complained of abdominal pains caused during the fingerprinting. He held his stomach and moaned loudly as they took him and the others to the Tombs jail.

The Tombs refused to accept the injured prisoners. So Pete and Paul carted their unhappy crew to Beekman Hospital, where the husband was fitted with a cast and crutches, and Sanchez was given pills, which he accepted quietly.

When Ronald Benson and Luis Navarro arrived at night court for the arraignment, they had to wait. To make matters worse, they were soon told to go home. Night court was the butt-end of New York City's absurdly overcrowded criminal courts system, and it routinely added the day's overflow to its own calendar, pushing *its* cases over to the following day. Benson, the hustler, professed disgust at this creaky and wholly inconvenient system of justice, and by 8 A.M. the next day, when he was supposed to reappear, he had dropped out of the case altogether.

That left Navarro, a thoroughly unhappy witness. The truckdriver had a thin mustache and scattered gold teeth, and he lived on Avenue D in a depressingly small flat with his wife and tribe of children. He was still angry at the indignities visited upon him, and he felt a vague civic duty to follow through with the case. But he was frightened. His neighborhood had begun to bristle with real or imagined threats from Sanchez's friends. And he quickly found that justice was expensive.

Sanchez's case never reached a full trial, but there were weeks and weeks of pretrial hearings beginning in late August, and they cost Navarro dearly. In one, the defense lawyers revealed that he was collecting welfare under another name—a common ghetto hustle, since neither welfare payments nor his bottom-rung job supported his family adequately. But the testimony cost him the welfare, and the hearings interferred with his job.

On any scheduled hearing day, he had to be in court at 8 A.M., often for nothing. In such nickel and dime cases, the defense routinely asks for adjournment after adjournment in the hope that witnesses will lose interest. Pete and Paul were paid to be there; Navarro lost at least half a day's pay each time.

And he was summoned to court often. He arrived each day in work clothes hoping to be finished in time for at least half a day's driving. But the day's proceedings prior to each adjournment often dragged into the afternoon, leaving him without wages. And the threats from Sanchez's friends mounted steadily. Navarro was given three dollars and fifty cents a day for lunch by the district attorney's office. He began to drink rye and ginger ale, skipping food.

Pete and Paul were told to provide him as much neighborhood protection as possible. They drove him to and from court appearances, and they told the sector car in his neighborhood about the trial. At lunch they tried to bolster his courage, buying him food when he drank through his city-supplied money. All went well until he decided to withdraw from the case altogether.

Benson, who was long gone, had left behind an affidavit swearing that Sanchez and his friends had wronged him in various ways, and this at least could be used to help support a grand jury indictment for felony robbery. Beyond that, Benson was no help; and this irritated Pete—a lot.

For he'd also failed to return Pete's five dollars. In the following months, Pete saw the short, flabby hustler occasionally, and these were moments of considerable tension. At first Pete was too proud to ask for the money. Then it became clear that Benson was purposely ignoring the subject, so Pete developed a sudden interest in his debtor's criminal record. He found that Benson's yellow sheet reached back a full ten years, featuring burglary, felony assault, criminal mischief, assault on a policeman, and repeated charges of possession of dangerous drugs.

"Hey, Ronnie, I wanta talk to you," Pete yelled out on 11th Street one day.

Benson, standing with two women, left them and followed Pete timidly into a hallway.

"Where's my five, Ronnie?"

"Oh yeah, man . . . uh . . ." Benson looked around him in the dark hallway and shifted uneasily on his feet. His arms were scabby with needle tracks, and the scar of an old stab wound had left fleshy ridges on his stomach. ". . . uh, I forgot about that, you know?"

Pete's hand jumped toward Benson's shirt pocket, closing around a greasy folded-over envelope. He ripped it open as the hustler watched in dismay, finding a lone joint.

"Hey, Ronnie," Pete mocked. "What's *this*?"

"Oh, yeah . . . uh." He was very nervous now. "Well, it's not mine, you know?"

"Hey, Ronnie," Pete almost laughed. "Put your hands behind your back. We're goin' in."

In the end, Pete's search was judged to lack sufficient "probable cause," and the arrest was thrown out. And he still hadn't collected his five dollars.

A few weeks later he spotted Benson again. Pete was with Paul, and they followed Benson to a shoe store on

Avenue B. It had rained that day, and the sidewalks were slippery. Paul loitered across the street while Pete walked to the store and waited outside.

Benson walked out and felt a hand reach for him. The hustler instinctively shoved it away and struck out at his unseen assailant with his umbrella. Pete ducked, lost his balance and fell.

Paul thought Pete had been attacked. He rushed across the street and fell on Benson with his sap as Pete pulled himself up from the sidewalk. Benson screamed and fought back, and Paul hit him until the hustler's blood fell all over the wet sidewalk.

"Help!" Benson screamed. "Help, these motherfuckers are killing me! Police brutality! Help!"

They called a radio car as he sat in a puddle of his own juices on the sidewalk. A crowd had gathered, and he was still yelling as they herded him into it.

In the station house, Pete kept a straight face and charged him with resisting arrest and assaulting a policeman.

Something quite strange happened now. Benson suddenly appeared to be convinced that *Pete* had beaten him. It was an odd, almost eerie turnabout that had happened to Pete and Paul before. By now they'd come to joke about it. Paul's baby-faced features made it difficult for people he had hurt moments earlier to blame him, and in their rage or pain they often focused on Pete, whose sad-clown face seemed to be a psychic lightning rod. Time after time, they decided that Pete, not Paul, had hurt them; that Pete alone was capable of explosive abuse of his police powers, not Paul.

In the squad room, Benson whimpered and bled and stared at Pete angrily. Then he pulled a crumpled five dollar bill from a side pocket and rubbed it in the half-dried blood on his head.

"Here's your blood money, motherfucker!"

Pete laughed, washed the bill and bought a couple of drinks at Cal's after work.

The lawyers made them laugh. There were three of them: a tall one, a middle-sized fellow and a small one. Inevitably, they appeared in the courtroom in formation, tall first, then middle, then small. Pete and Paul named them Hart, Schaffner and Marx, exploding in silent laughter.

In the matter of courtroom procedure, the lawyers were not funny at all. Loaned to Legal Aid by three Wall Street law firms, they demonstrated a methodical, almost dogged pursuit of freedom for their unsavory clients. Pete knew that the case against Sanchez was virtually closed; he suspected they knew it, too. Still, they made all the motions he could have imagined—and then some—and made them again and again in a vain effort to open the cage that he and Paul and a young district attorney named McNulty had constructed.

The hearings lasted more than six weeks, and Navarro seemed more frightened each day. He'd begun to drink more and more; he had complained bitterly of the money he was losing. And then he disappeared.

"He doesn't live here anymore," Navarro's wife told them

when they arrived one morning to pick him up. Blank-faced children swirled about her skirts, and she said nothing more.

A few days later, they found him in an apartment several blocks away. He said he'd "changed jobs," and he explained nothing else. They talked about the case, and he looked at them unhappily and agreed to go back.

A frightening connection, meanwhile, was developing between Sanchez and Pete.

The gunman had begun watching Pete. His small red eyes seemed to smoulder at Pete across the room. Through the early hearings, the gunman sat impassively among his friends. But on a Wednesday, Sanchez had suddenly turned in his chair, swiveling full around. He began staring at Pete. From that morning on, his gaze was focused with the the intensity of a heat lamp.

He watched no one else. Pete sat several rows in back of him, and now each day Sanchez rotated slowly into position to look directly into Pete's eyes, locking on Pete as if the eyes were handcuffs, holding as Pete shifted uncomfortably on the wooden courtroom seat. It began to seem to Pete as if no one else was in the room, as if the entire courtroom was plunged into darkness and he and Sanchez were alone in some kind of duel.

Pete hated being watched. During his first days on the avenue, he'd become convinced that groups of people he heard chattering in Spanish were watching him. It bothered Pete. It had always bothered him. It bothered him so much that he enrolled in a night school Spanish course so he could translate what they were saying. He dropped the classes because they proved time-consuming, but he retained that self-conscious feeling. He was plagued by it.

And now he saw Sanchez and his friends whispering in that same language. They were talking about him. He *knew* it. And when they finished talking, Sanchez inevitably turned and looked at him. Sanchez's eyes burrowed into Pete as if to drill a hole in him.

Pete forced himself to stare back, returning the venom, but the gunman stared relentlessly. It began to seem that Sanchez was watching him for entire morning or afternoon sessions, aiming his hatred like a spotlight.

And then one day Sanchez extended his forefinger and made his hand into a symbolic gun. He turned in his seat as if he owned the courtroom and extended his arm and pointed the "gun" at Pete's face, holding it for several long seconds—depressing his thumb slowly.

His lips moved quickly, forming a small mimick explosion. Sanchez shot Pete repeatedly as the courtroom days passed. Each blast sent a psychic bullet between Pete's eyes. And each time, Pete felt it a little more, as if he was condemned to sit on the wooden courtroom seat endlessly dodging bullets.

He began to look for excuses to catch Sanchez alone. And hit him. When he and Paul were detailed to take the prisoners back to their cells, he waited for a moment when no one was watching and smacked Sanchez on the back of his head with his open hand. He hoped Sanchez would retaliate, giving him an excuse to use his fists or his club.

"I'm gonna get you, motherfucker," Sanchez growled.

It was all he would say, but it was effective. In the custody of other cops or courtroom guards, he'd say it again, mocking Pete as he passed by.

"I'm gonna *get* you, motherfucker."

For he seemed to sense something in Pete, a fear he could exploit, a self-loathing so far down as to be almost invisible. He went after it like a jackal seeking dead flesh. He kept up the pressure, the eyes staring, the forefinger and cocked thumb, the whispered threats. Pete had been threatened by other felons, but not like this, not so systematically.

"I'm gonna *get* you, motherfucker."

Pete wanted very much to hurt him.

The testimony lasted nearly six weeks into late September, and at the end of it, after some bargaining at the bench between the prosecution and defense lawyers, the presiding judge agreed to find the defendant guilty of second-degree felony robbery, dropping the gun charge.

At the sentencing in October, he gave Sanchez two to five years. The gunman leapt from his chair and turned toward Pete once more.

"I'm gonna *kill* you!" he screamed. His startled lawyers looked up as he reached for something on the table.

Pete jumped out of his seat as if it were spring-loaded. He rushed forward, thinking Sanchez was about to throw something, *hoping* for it, lusting to plant a fist in Sanchez's face with all the justification a police officer can muster when attacked by the other side.

Courtroom guards stepped between them, locking Sanchez in handcuffs and forcing Pete back.

Pete watched as they took him away, leaving what seemed to him an oddly empty space in the room, a sense of unfinished business as he stood before the courtroom railing. He looked at Sanchez's empty chair, and even the emptiness of it cut into him. He was deeply shocked at what had happened, and he recoiled. He always got on with people—even people he arrested. He was proud of that. He *needed* it. It was as if Victorio Sanchez's threats had driven a knife into him.

Paul reached for his hand. Pete returned his partner's handclasp vigorously. They had wanted this conviction; they'd wanted it badly. It could have been an easy gun conviction, costing Sanchez less than a year, but they knew enough about him to want more. Call it justice. Call it revenge. It was their longest trial, one of their best arrests. It was reason to celebrate.

CHAPTER 6

As a teen-ager, Pete came to understand the effect of *watching* someone. In high school he courted his future wife, Helen Woodrow, in a conspiratorial and jealous fashion, spying on her constantly. They met on a school boat ride after Pete's junior year, and by the following winter they were a steady item.

Helen was quite taken with Pete, but at first she remained aloof. "I sort of felt he was just a guy I was going steady with," she remembers. "I had three boy friends on the side, and I was still seeing them because I wasn't ready to settle down." She smiles. "They might call when he was there, and he'd get on the phone and say bad things. He was very jealous."

An understatement. At parties, Pete ripped down curtains, knocked over furniture, and picked fights when other boys asked Helen to dance. Some nights he traveled half-drunk to Brooklyn to watch people go in and out of her apartment building. If he recognized a rival, he threatened him.

And he called Helen. And called. And called.

"He was getting on my nerves. I couldn't go shopping with my sister. He'd call my mother. Where is she? He'd call every hour. My mother finally said are you going to marry this guy or what? He's driving me crazy with the phone. So I told Pete it would be better if we saw less of each other."

Pete pushed harder. He called just as often. He drove to Brooklyn just as regularly. And he threatened her other boy friends. And then he added his touch of psychological warfare. "His men" were watching her, he said. "They wore white trench coats."

"Get *serious*," she said.

"What about today?"

"What about it?"

"My men were watching you."

"Come on!"

"You see anybody in a white trench coat?"

"Well . . . yes."

"All right."

Helen never quite fell for it, but the stories unnerved her. He told the stories deadpan. Watch for the white raincoats, he insisted.

And she finally gave in. After that they were together constantly. They were friends as well as lovers, for most of all Pete needed her friendship.

"I don't think anybody has a *lot* of friends," he will say when pressed on the issue. "A lot of people know a lot of people. But that's all." He had broken with Tommy Ryan at this time. "When I lost Tommy, I started looking for someone else, and I got seriously involved with Helen. I had no one else to lean on. She was my girlfriend, and she was my best friend. She was everything."

Pete's break with Tommy Ryan was caused by an auto accident.

In the late hours after Tommy's senior prom, Tommy and Pete went out drinking in Tommy's new car, a Pontiac Bonneville. About 2 A.M. Tommy became drowsy and climbed into the back seat to sleep. Pete took the wheel. He was seventeen, carrying a junior operator's license.

A warm spring night. The streets were still alive, and traffic was heavy as Pete moved the wheel of the big car in and out of traffic, happily buzzed. No sound came from the back seat.

It hit him from the left side. He saw nothing—maybe he drove into it—but in the next instant everything exploded around him, all ripping metal and squealing rubber with a sickening hollow crash at the end as the Bonneville gave its all to a steel light pole. He saw blood on his jacket. He walked out.

Tommy lay in a drunken stupor in the back. Several hours passed before doctors knew that he would not go into a coma.

Pete managed to convince the police that Tommy had been driving even though he was found in the back seat. He waited while they filled out their forms, then went to the hospital to tell Tommy the same thing. And Tommy, having no memory of what had led to the accident, believed his best friend. The accident was officially noted and transcribed as if Tommy had been at the wheel, and the insurance adjustors were so advised.

Tommy lay in the hospital in considerable pain. He had no collision insurance and nothing was left of his car.

Bill Bon Viso came to him and quietly offered to pay off the car loan.

At first Tommy didn't understand. Then he turned away from Pete's father in disgust. He would take care of his own obligations. Where was Pete? Why did his father have to take care of it?

Eventually Pete came to him and admitted he'd been driving. He hadn't wanted to upset Tommy by telling him a different story than he'd told the police, he said lamely. Shortly afterward, Tommy joined the Army.

They still see each other. But it isn't the same.

Rose Bon Viso began the Sunday mornings of Pete's childhood by mixing spices, sausage, canned tomatoes and pork skins into a sauce which simmered all day on the stove, filling the apartment with a heavy fragrance. She prepared the bread, salad and vegetables, then arranged heaping bowls of spaghetti, macaroni and pasta shells for the table. The rest of the family, which by 1965 unofficially included Helen, gathered in mid-afternoon, sitting down after Bill had opened a large bottle of dark red wine. The meal lasted most of the afternoon, and later that night the sauce would be reheated and bread and leftover meat brought out.

Sundays were very special to Pete, but holidays, which were Sundays written large, fairly glistened. Something in

Pete's father asserted itself grandly on those days. It was Bill Bon Viso's nature to play host.

He designed the holidays as occasions to end family discord, a time to drink deep and let old quarrels die or at least leave them at the doorstep. For blood ties and friendship mattered a great deal to Bill. It mattered that his home be full, and it mattered that his family was together. Pete, too, was hooked on holidays. He watched his mother create the meals passed down to her over so many generations, and he listened to his father laugh with the uncles, aunts and cousins. And he smiled knowingly as Bill made one excuse after another to go to the kitchen for the jug of Manhattans prepared a month ahead and left to age on the kitchen shelf.

As the years passed, it was clear that Bill wanted to limit the aging process to his Manhattans. When Pete was a teenager, his father began using Dr. Small's hair coloring. He kept a full head of hair until his death, but the graying was an intolerable sign of age, and once a week he combed in the dye, counting the wrinkles on his forehead and the crow's feet gathering around his eyes as he did. He'd joked over the years that they came from frowning at his "little guy," whom he now called "big guy." But he could not hide the fact that he was getting old, and this did not suit his vanity. His neck sagged; he began to register a growing loss of weight. And he refused to see a doctor even for routine checkups.

And still, he kept his leg hidden.

The artificial limb had changed from wood to plastic over the years. It began at his thigh and had a metal joint allowing him to bend it at its simulated knee. To attach the leg each morning, he pulled a woolen stump stocking over his flesh. Then he inserted his covered thigh into a saddle-like space at the top of the leg. The leg had canvas straps which stretched up to and over his shoulder. Once the leg was fitted, he adjusted the straps until he was comfortable for the day.

Pete remembers one of those days, a Sunday when Bill had to work at the warehouse. He'd come home for Sunday dinner; Helen was with them.

After dessert and coffee, Bill left the third floor apartment and walked downstairs to go across the street. It was the family's custom to wave to him from the window as he headed back, but today he suddenly turned in the middle of the road, raised his hand and whistled urgently at them. He called for Pete.

It turned out that Bill's strap had snapped, and he needed his son's help to get to the other side of the sreet without having the leg fall off. They shuffled toward the family car, which was parked at the opposite curb.

Pete helped his father into the front seat and asked what else he could do. Bill was embarrassed because Helen was in the house; he asked his son to sneak another leg out.

Pete climbed the stairs and whispered to Rose. She nodded, and she and one of Pete's half-sisters maneuvered Helen from the kitchen into another room as Pete slipped into his parents' bedroom and pulled another of Bill's false legs from the closet. He wrapped it in a blanket like a corpse and rushed downstairs. It mattered enormously to him that no one, including Helen, be embarrassed.

Bill's nature was to keep nearly everything inside. He

rarely discussed a bad day at work, preferring to suppress his frustrations. "Whatsa matter with him?" Rose might say to the rest of the house as he walked through the kitchen. Nothing. She'd ask again. Silence. Bill would settle sullenly into his chair to read the paper, and in twenty minutes he would be father to his house again, humorous and warm. It was unlikely he would talk of the day's incident at all.

"I thought it was terrific," Pete once observed. "You shouldn't burden other people with your problems, you know? If they are causing them, okay. But if it's your problem, there's no reason to put it on someone else."

Pete lived by this idea. He carried it into his adult life, into police work, into his marriage.

The old, over-stuffed chair in the living room had a hassock beside it. It was generally acknowledged to be Bill's chair, part of a lime-green living room set matched by an overstuffed couch. He sat in it to read and watch television, propping his artificial leg on the hassock, settling back, quiet, calm.

A week short of his nineteenth birthday, Pete approached Bill as he sat in the chair to ask guidance on the question of marrying Helen. In reality, Pete wasn't asking permission. He knew his parents liked her enormously, and that they expected a marriage. But he wanted to show respect.

"Dad, I think I'd like to marry Helen," the son said. "I'd like to get engaged to her on my birthday—what do you think?"

Bill beamed and looked up happily from the chair. "She's a wonderful girl, son. I wish you all the world's luck."

Rose had planned to ask some people over for Pete's birthday that Sunday. It was decided that the last gift would be for Helen.

Pete bought a 97-point blue Marquis diamond, three points short of a full carat, a rock people would *notice* It cost more than $900, an enormous amount of money for an $80-a-week police trainee. But his career was set, and soon he would change to the blue uniform and begin steady pay raises and promotions. He would have a wife and family, a home, and he would have respect. He would not be part of any shape-up labor gang at the Fulton Fish Market, like his grandfather and so many of his teen-age friends. He would not be among the street people lounging on park benches outside his mother's window. He would leave the housing projects behind—the diamond would be proof of it.

"Here, you open this," he said to Helen at the end of Sunday's dinner.

It was hard to tell whether Helen or the ring sparkled more.

They planned to wait a year for the wedding, but they began looking for a reception hall almost immediately. Bill and Rose wanted a large wedding, and so the young couple finally settled on a hall large enough for 300 people. They made arrangements for a 90-minute cocktail hour, a dinner featuring prime ribs and two bottles of champagne on each table, and a five-piece band for dancing.

Underneath, Helen was frightened. "I don't want him to be a cop," she cried to her mother one day. Helen remembered her father's drinking, the tragic death. But when the older woman suggested she talk to Pete, Helen knew it was impossible. Even now he planned to become a detective. Already, as a gray-uniformed clerk, he loved what he did.

And already, she had nightmares of his death. He was everything to her, her future, her family. She imagined becoming a widow. She thought of him dying, bleeding in some ghetto alley. She couldn't bear the thought of waiting each day for the rest of her life, wondering if he was coming home. Yet she knew she would have to endure this fear. She knew he would not listen.

For her fiance thought his future sublime as he sat at the ancient telephone switchboard in a musty police office in his gray junior-cop uniform. He wouldn't be a real cop until his 21st birthday, but then he would be an active cop, one who made *quality* arrests. He knew the streets of his childhood, he knew the people who lived in them. He would be that kind of cop.

Every Sunday now, Helen carried her portable record player and a scratched 45 rpm recording of the tune *More* to the Bon Viso apartment. Slowly, carefully, she was teaching Bill Bon Viso to dance.

And each Sunday he retreated immediately to his corner chair. Slowly, she coaxed him out of it, pleading tenderly, telling him what it would mean to her on her wedding day, stroking his vanity with a soft, sure touch. And since he adored the coltish girl reaching out to him, Bill relented, despite his leg. Helen would bring the pride of a big family wedding to his household, something his daughters had denied him, and this was important to him.

For his daughters had simply announced their marriages at home. No nervous suitors came around. No one asked for "guidance." Nothing was done the old way. They had civil ceremonies in judges' chambers, and Bill, showing no emotion, quietly agreed each time.

He was deeply pleased that Pete's wedding would be different. If Helen had her way, Bill and Rose would dance with the young couple in front of nearly 300 people while the band played a song that promised eternal happiness. The song would *last* an eternity, he thought. He hadn't danced in his life.

But his new daughter was patient. She coaxed him onto his feet; she taught him to move and sway to the music. And then she put Rose into his arms. The dancing was awkward at first, difficult for Rose as well. But in the end, Helen made him do what he wanted to do, and he was secretly pleased.

Pete and Helen were married in October of 1968. It was a Saturday of gentle breezes and rich Autumn colors, and Pete and Bill and a neighborhood friend Pete asked to be his best man climbed into their tuxedos at the Bon Viso apartment, adjusting suspenders and tying each others' bow ties. Bill uncorked a bottle of rye and poured three drinks. He proposed the first of many toasts that day to his son, and the three men touched their glasses and drank deeply.

The older man looked around the apartment to be sure Rose couldn't see him, and he reached into his pocket for an envelope. He stepped forward quickly and stuffed it into Pete's vest pocket.

"Two tickets to Puerto Rico," he said quite seriously—

only the aging laugh lines around his mouth gave him away. "You can be on the plane in half an hour." And he broke out laughing, catching himself, pouring another drink for his son and his son's best man.

They drank the rye straight and called to Rose and went downstairs where a limousine waited. An hour later, after a few more drinks at a neighborhood bar, Pete walked nervously to the altar of the All Saints Church in Brooklyn and stood in front of it somewhat drunkenly as guests filed into the pews. The music started. Helen, draped in shimmering white lace, stepped from a side door. She was radiant, as if reborn. The priest made motions and spoke words, and before Pete could believe it, he was married.

When they arrived at the reception hall after a stop for photographs, hundreds of wellwishers were already drinking cocktails. They went to a smaller room for champagne, and a maitre d' explained that the flower girl would enter the ballroom first, followed by ushers and bridesmaids. Each would be introduced to applause. The maid of honor best man would be next, followed by the parents of the bride and groom.

Then:

"Ladies and gentlemen, for the first time in public, Mr. and Mrs. Peter Bon Viso!"

Double doors swept open and triumphant music filled the cavernous room. Pete and Helen walked proudly toward the dance floor and their future, and the room came to its feet, exploding in applause. The band struck up *More* and the young couple danced in a spotlight, joined soon by their wedding party.

"And now," the maitre d' announced, "the parents of the groom will join them."

It was the crowning moment. After a lifetime of awkwardness and concealed shame, all of Bill and Rose Bon Viso's world watched, applauding, drinking champagne, enjoying the bounty Bill and Rose had provided. The old couple felt warm and flushed. A generation of struggle, bitterness and joy was passed on now, and they took their rightful bows. The music of this day belonged as much to them as to their son and daughter-in-law. They were young and in love again.

Years later when so much had changed, the wedding album offered ghostly, ironic impressions of that night. Some of the studio photos had been taken prankishly; Helen held a rolling pin in one of them, a chain was attached to Pete's nose in another. But the most striking photos were of Pete and his father. In them, the two men clasped hands. The father wore a black bow tie, the son's tie was white. The son was several inches taller, and he stood beside his father with his jaw set pridefully pushing out. The pictures show a classically stereotyped Italian face —the well-oiled tough guy look Pete had worked so hard over the years to perfect. Bill Bon Viso offered the camera a more relaxed image; a warm, slightly worldly countenance, an aging father together with his harvest, a man whose only son had been married this day under joyous and honorable circumstances.

Bill Bon Viso was as happy that day as he ever would be.

CHAPTER 7

THE Brooklyn apartment was small, but it was a beginning. The newlyweds felt they had started well. Helen had found a secretary's job on Wall Street, and Pete was scheduled to graduate to his blue uniform, which meant a pay raise. And their cash wedding gifts totaled more than $3000.

Helen's mother had found them a rent-controlled apartment in her building for $57 a month. It needed work, but Pete and Helen were cozy enough. He put in carpeting, linoleum and wallpaper, and they developed an easy, neighborly relationship with the older woman. On Sundays, Mary Woodrow brought bagels and cream cheese and the papers across the building's courtyard, and she and her daughter talked over coffee while Pete sat in an easy chair and watched television. They'd bought a washing machine with some of the wedding money. Helen usually put the wash in before she left for Wall Street in the mornings; and Pete, working four to twelve, hung it outside. If he forgot to take it down, which happened often, Mary tended to things. At night, Helen would find a basket of folded clothes in the apartment.

The older woman gave them a hide-a-bed sofa. Bill and Rose bought them a walnut-paneled bar that Pete had admired in a wholesale shop. "You go to the movies when you're a kid," he explained once, "and you see a boss or somebody having people in his apartment. He serves them drinks from his bar, you know?" It was part of the dream.

They had extra money, which allowed Pete to indulge both sides of his financial psyche. On his sensible side, he joined with a friend and bought land in Godeffroy, New York. The acreage included two half-finished cottages, which gave both men and their families weekend places. Later, Pete bought a two-family house with tenants on Long Island, and he became a landlord.

The reckless side of Pete's finances was his father's legacy, gambling. He'd begun to frequent neighborhood card games even before graduating from high school, often at the Alley Boys Club on Pike Street. The stakes were one to five—meaning that you put one dollar in the pot to start and could bet up to five on the last card.

As a cop, he avoided the neighborhood games. Drugs were sometimes involved, and he could no longer afford that kind of trouble. This limitation didn't slow him down, of course; he found games within the force. He began to gamble regularly with other Ninth Precinct cops. The stakes slowly got higher. At one point he was $1200 in debt to

Jerry Bono, still his best friend on the force after Paul. He'd had a bad run at the tables, and he wasn't doing all that well with his bookie. Jerry finally took pity on him. He challenged him to eight-ball at Cal's and lost purposely all afternoon at fifty dollars a game. In return for such charity, Pete picked up Jerry's restaurant tabs for more than a year.

He'd also gotten heavily into sports betting. For several years, football was a highly profitable sideline for the young cop. In 1973, he won more than $2400, doubling his money at the last minute on a flamboyant $1400 superbowl bet.

He *liked* risks. At the poker tables, he might easily drop fifty dollars into the pot to fill an inside straight. He was a gambler in every sense of the word. "You go to win," his father once told him. "If you do, it's the greatest feeling in the world. But you expect to lose, too—and you take it well."

If the inside straight failed in its uphill climb to beat the table's odds, the other players would hardly know from Pete's face, which might pale briefly. After that he might be a little . . . more quiet, that was all. He also followed basktball games, betting between $50 and $300 on games he liked. "If I wasn't doing anything else, and I wanted to watch a game on television," he once explained, "I'd throw a few bucks on it to give me some interest." One wintry season he lost more than $3000 and quietly gave up the sport.

He didn't like the track ("I've seen too many people that knew a lot about horses go broke") or baseball ("The lines are crazy—they can go to a point where you hafta lay down eighty dollars to win fifty if you want the favorite, it gets outta hand"), so he stayed with fooball and poker. They were enough, if one be heavily as he did, to keep most men on edge.

And the stakes were rising. Poker within the police department was nothing like the one-to-five games at the Alley Boys Club. Eventually he got into a Thursday night game where the bets ranged between $50 and $200 on a single card. A pot hight have more than $1000 in it. And it made no sense to walk into the game with less than $1500. As a result, the game needed fresh blood regularly. The stakes were simply too high; players washed out every month. Even here, Pete remained reckless to a fault. He was luckier than most of the regulars, and he managed to stay in the game for several years. His father would have been pleased.

November, 1969: a cool, relatively quiet Saturday night. Pete rode that night with the "Admiral," a cop who'd spent 20 years in the Navy before joining the force.

It was after ten, and they were cruising slowly down Second Avenue. The radio buzzed and squawked as usual. Then without knowing why, Pete felt his head jerk toward it in half-conscious recognition. He realized that he was listening to a Fifth Precinct call, ". . . difficulty breathing . . ." with a familiar address: 20 Catherine Slip, Apartment 2-C.

Pete grabbed the microphone, suddenly frightened. He asked the dispatcher to repeat the call. Again: 20 Catherine Slip, Apartment 2-C.

"It's my mother's house," he almost shouted, his hands shaking as he replaced the microphone. "Let's go!"

He knew as they rode that Bill had been losing weight for more than a year. As the weight loss had continued, he and Rose had finally overruled the old man's protests and had taken him to a doctor. The physician immediately recognized a diabetic problem; he also found other irregularities of old age and prescribed a variety of pills and diet changes.

Pete saw a Fifth Precinct car in front, and he rushed up the back stairs to find two cops in his father's bedroom. The old man lay on his bed, ashen-faced, struggling desperately to breathe. Rose stood in a corner off to one side, silent in her fear. The cops told Pete that an emergency service car, which carried oxygen, was coming, and Pete stood over his father and waited for a long, dark moment until the car arrived. With oxygen, the older man's death mask fell away. An ambulance was called, and he was taken to Beekman Hospital with Pete and Rose following behind.

But at 62, Bill Bon Viso was still proud. When a Beekman doctor suggested he stay for a few days, he petulantly refused. Pete and Rose argued on the doctor's side, but the old man demanded to be taken home.

As a result, Pete agreed to take Rose home in the radio car and return after his shift ended at midnight. Bill Bon Viso looked hard at his son. If Pete didn't return, the old man vowed, he'd take a cab home himself, pajamas and all.

At midnight, Pete brought him street clothes, a wheelchair and crutches, the latter since Bill, in the emergency, hadn't had time to put on his artificial leg. Driving back, Pete asked the older man several times if he might be upset about anything.

"No, no," his father said, lapsing each time into silence.

At the projects, Pete drove up on the sidewalk. He ran ahead to check the building's lobby to make certain it was empty. Then he ran back to the car to help Bill into the wheelchair. In the darkness he hurriedly pushed his father between the car and the elevator. They rose one floor, and Pete pushed him down the dismal hallway to apartment 2-C.

Inside, safe from prying eyes, Bill seemed content. He thanked Pete for his help, and Pete left the apartment and went home to Brooklyn.

In the morning, the older man turned to his wife and said that he was deeply upset. How could she call for help, he asked, without giving him time to put on his leg? She was not to do it again, under *any* circumstances. If it should happen again that he had trouble breathing, God forbid, he wanted time to put it on before she went to the telephone. Was that understood?

Rose listened to the man she loved so deeply and nodded gravely at the instructions.

Two weeks passed.

The call came to Brooklyn at 6:30 A.M. Again, it was Saturday.

"Pete, it's your father!" Rose's voice fairly vibrated with fear. "Come right away!"

"Ma, what is it?"

"The same thing. He won't let me call the police. He said to call you—for you to come over right now."

Pete doesn't remember the ride. He doesn't remember getting dressed, or starting his car. On normal days he is a careless, irresponsible driver: he speeds excessively, changes lanes impulsively, ignores stop signs. A red light in Pete's path has a fifty-fifty chance of being obeyed in any kind of traffic.

He made it to Catherine Slip in half the usual time.

And he found his father dying. Bill's face was the color of gray smoke rising from a sputtering fire. He gagged taking in air. His voice seemed to float away in the suddenly large room.

In a frail whisper the old man asked his wife to leave the room. He was barely able to form the words.

"Dad, I'm calling an ambulance," Pete blurted out as his mother walked toward the kitchen.

"All right." The voice seemed very small. "But you help me get dressed."

Pete ran to the kitchen phone, dialed 911 and asked for an ambulance and emergency service. And he put down the phone thinking everything would be all right. He went in the bedroom to help his father.

Bill asked for his leg, which was next to the bed. Pete brought it over, and Bill tried to sit up. Pete held him by his arms and shoulders now, lifting him gently.

Then something changed. The old man's eyes flickered like a candle flame, and he lurched forward. He vomited, he wet himself, and he fell against Pete, who still held his shoulders. And Pete knew his father was dead.

He began to cry softly, letting the old man down just as two emergency service cops entered the bedroom. One rushed over and put his mouth on Bill's mouth and began exhaling heavily into him in a rising and falling rhythm. The other cop pounded Bill's chest. Rose remained quietly in the kitchen.

Then, as if only Pete knew what had already happened,

ambulance attendants arrived and methodically put the quiet old man on a stretcher, carrying him slowly downstairs as the two cops continued to work on him. In the ambulance the attendants gave Bill oxygen and continued pumping his chest; and at the hospital he was taken to a room where a machine helped work his chest and pump even more oxygen into him.

In about 10 minutes, a doctor came to Pete. He said he was very sorry.

Pete walked mindlessly back to Catherine Slip. He remembers nothing about the walk or the kind of day it was. He was his father's son; and now the flesh and spirit of half his life was gone.

He walked into the apartment. Rose waited in the kichen, cowering and silent. Before he could say anything, she started to cry. For a while, they held each other, and finally she went to the phone and called her sister, telling her to call the rest of the family. Pete then called the Ninth Precinct and spoke to a lieutenant at the desk, asking for time off.

Later that day, he and an uncle went to a neighborhood funeral home to make the necessary arrangements.

That night he thought of something else. Why hadn't he called emergency service from *Brooklyn?*

The question began to turn over and over in his mind like an animal tortured by fire. Why hadn't he called 911 *after his mother called him?* Why hadn't he called to say he was a cop and that he needed help?

The questions rushed at him like bullets: why hadn't he told Helen to do it, Helen who lay in bed beside him and knew what was happening as well as anyone.

How foolish he was! He could have saved his father, but in his hurry to be a dutiful son, he had failed to be a man! How simple to disobey his father that morning and call for help!

The emergency service cops, who came too late anyway, had compounded things by telling him he'd called just as they stepped out of their car—precious seconds away from the radio. If Pete had called a few minutes earlier. . . .

Pete went over and over the morning. Why didn't he insist that his father lie still and wait for the oxygen? He hadn't wanted to excite him by not helping, he told himself. Why didn't he make the old man move more slowly? But Bill was stubborn: he insisted on being fully dressed. So why hadn't he *disobeyed* his father? It came down to that. And he knew the answer.

For above all he'd wanted to please him. It was so crazy—pleasing him meant killing him. That's what it came down to. He'd had a decision to make that morning, and he'd made the wrong one. He looked at his father in the funeral home that night, recoiling at the sight of the old man's face closed in a ghastly, powdered death mask, and he knew that, under pressure, he'd failed. A man had one or two really important decisions to make in his life. He'd blown this one.

It was all too complicated. He looked at Rose, a woman who had spent her life defying pain, and something in him wondered. What did she think of him now? Did *she* blame him, too? He would spend the rest of his life thinking about this. Should he be punished? He just didn't know.

CHAPTER 8

IT was impossible, he knew it was, but Pete had just seen Victorio Sanchez on a subway platform. It was early April of 1973, about six months after the sentencing.

Sanchez *had* to be in jail. He belonged to the past, nothing more. Yet someone—someone who looked strikingly like the gunman—had just now stepped out of a subway car in a crowd of rush-hour commuters. Pete stood open-mouthed on the platform watching him climb the station stairs.

Pete was on a routine assignment for the district attorney's office. He wore civilian clothes, and he stood near the tracks telling himself it was a mistake. But he was stunned at the man's astonishing resemblance to the gunman, who had to be in jail. He knew that the lawyers had made no serious attempt to appeal Sanchez's case, and there was no talk of bail. Sanchez was *doing time;* he was very far away. He was supposed to have gone to Auburn State Prison, a maximum security fortress in the far upper reaches of New York state where cons did very hard time. He had no hope of parole for at least two years.

Pete told himself all this. But then he prided himself on his memory for faces. A dozen years earlier, a man named Sy had run a delicatessen near the housing projects. Pete bought Cokes and sandwiches there, and he and Sy exchanged routine pleasantries. One winter Sy closed up shop and left, retiring to Long Island. There was nothing special in his and Pete's relationship. The man was part of Pete's neighborhood, a familiar face.

Ten years later, Pete was eating in a Long Island diner when he saw that same face. He thought a moment, and he walked over to say hello. Sy was surprised; it took him a moment to bring Pete into focus, which didn't bother Pete at all. Most people's memories were not as good as his.

And today he was on a subway platform waiting for the uptown train, and he saw the dark bulldog face. He saw the short muscular man emerge from a crowded car and climb the stairs toward daylight.

Pete ran toward the crowd of commuters, leaping up the stairs as they disappeared around a landing. When he reached the top, Sanchez was gone. He stood a moment and thought about what he might have seen, and what it meant.

He thought about Sanchez the rest of the morning. In the end, he kept the thoughts to himself. If Sanchez had escaped from prison, he reasoned, the department would have been notified. And *he* would have been notified, particularly since Sanchez had talked so often and so stridently of revenge.

Pete concluded that he'd seen someone else. He kept his fear inside.

Two months passed. He saw Sanchez again!

Pete was standing in front of Abie's, where he had been invited in for a drink. Paul had been assigned to fill a radio car seat, and Pete was alone. Pete hated being alone.

It was an afternoon late in May. He decided to let the drink pass. He and Abie stood and talked, and as they talked, Pete noticed a small group of Puerto Ricans walking on the other side of the street. They came into focus on the edge of his vision.

It was his job to watch people, particularly small groups in a hurry who might be carrying weapons or stolen household goods. Or someone who might be running from a warrant. Without actively thinking about it, he was checking them out.

He saw Sanchez looking at him.

It happened fast. The dark face jumped at him from the group of men. Sanchez's eyes reached out to him, vaulting the space across the street, and Pete stood transfixed in the man's gaze, caught between conflicting thoughts.

It *couldn't* be him. There was no logical reason why Victorio Sanchez should be walking the streets of New York, none, no reason why he should be free. He's not out, Pete said almost aloud. He can't be!

Yet Pete knew he was looking at Sanchez. He couldn't be mistaken, could he? He had a flawless memory for faces. And this time the man was looking back, staring at him with all the hatred Pete remembered from the hearings. Sanchez wore his usual black clothing, swung his short muscular arms, watched Pete, clearly waiting for his chance to . . . do what?

Disbelief won out briefly. Pete turned back to Abie, but he lost his composure quickly. "That was Sanchez," he blurted out.

The significance of this was lost on Abie, who hadn't followed the case. Abie started to say something, but Pete turned away again.

He saw the back of Sanchez's head as the small group reached the corner and went around it, disappearing.

He said goodby to Abie and walked down the avenue deep in thought.

"Now look," he muttered half aloud. "This is crazy. It *ain't* him."

And he walked on, waving to people he knew, adjusting his good soldier's mask and tending to business as he chewed on the problem underneath. It was a warm, crowded evening. He would visit people, tend his post and have dinner, flirt with the local girls, keep moving. He decided not to tell Paul.

"It ain't *him*," he said, startled at his own voice.

Three years after his father's death, Pete had moved to Long Island to be closer to Paul.

At first, he'd resisted changing his life so radically. He was a city boy. He had no interest in the suburbs. But Paul and Catherine had visited Godeffroy so often that they insisted the Bon Visos try a weekend on Long Island.

As a come-on, Paul bragged that fresh clams could be found near his house just by digging your toes in the sandy seashore.

Pete scoffed at this, but a barefoot expedition produced so many clams that they bought a cooler to take them home. Until that moment, all the clams in Pete's life had come from the Fulton Fish Market. He was delighted and amazed with this new world. That night they ate the clams with barbecued steaks in Paul's backyard, and Pete began to see suburbia with new eyes.

The following morning Paul told him that a house down the block was for sale. It had been repossessed, and it was empty and unkempt, junk strewn about, grass untended. But it was a bargain—and it was a *home,* not a $57-a-month apartment. Paul urged him to look at it.

Pete saw no reason to bother. He couldn't imagine leaving the city. He was nine minutes by car from his job. He was near his mother, and he had extra money because of the low rent.

But Helen pestered him. And since Paul was behind the idea, Pete agreed. Paul called a real estate office and arranged a tour that afternoon.

"The grass in the back yard was about a foot high," Pete remembered later. "The house was a dirty gray color, like it hadn't been painted in years. The paint was chipping off and the garage had water damage. I said to myself, how the fuck do they expect to sell this house?"

Inside Pete found moldy desolation. In the kitchen, the sink was broken. A rusty washing machine sat sullenly nearby filled with rotting clothes, sneakers, and empty beer cans.

"It looked like some sort of animal had gone to the bathroom in there."

The stove and refrigerator were decrepit, and when Pete walked into the living room, he found the breezeway door broken. The living room walls were filthy, the plasterboard in the back rooms was broken through. The stairway was badly scuffed, and most of the rooms had cheap tile on the floor. Some of the tiles were missing. Pete saw cat hair everywhere; some parts of the house smelled strongly of urine.

"You realize, of course, all this is going to be repaired and painted," the salesman said.

What a fucking wreck this house is, Pete thought.

Driving back to Manhattan, he discovered that Helen had been converted.

"Do you want our children to grow up in *Brooklyn?*" she said. Helen talked on of barbecues and picnics, green grass and the nearby schoolyards. She planned curtains and decorations, and talked of a swimming pool. And they'd be raising the children in a "nice" neighborhood. The Brooklyn apartment, after all, was practically on the edge of a ghetto. Within days, even Rose Bon Viso gave her okay. By the weekend, Pete had decided to buy it.

He closed the sale in October of 1972.

The house cost $22,500. The Veteran's Administration held the foreclosed mortgage, so it was happy to write a second one even though Pete was no veteran. He put down $3000 and committed himself to pay $210 a month for twenty-five years. To raise money for the remodeling, he sold his house and land in Godeffroy.

More than anything else, the restoration symbolized Pete's dream. He planned to rebuild the house with his hands, raising its beams with the help of friends and neighbors, planting solid roots in the community where he would live and educate his children.

He stole the lumber for his interior work by raiding Long Island Railroad work yards at night.

He began the renovation by raising the dormer. Paul offered to help, and Paul's brother, a building contractor, came by. They ripped out rafters and shingles, framed out two-by-four beams to form the dormer's walls, raised two-by-sixes for ceiling rafters, and covered everything with plywood. The dormer was a room now.

They rolled tar paper across the new roof and laid down shingles—and soon Pete began to feel an enormous pride. He began stepping back, like a sculptor, to admire his creation. Siding shingles followed, and as Pete worked around the outside of his changing house with a hammer and big nails, he was very aware of himself. Neighbors walked by, looking up. Pete fairly glowed.

As the sales contract specified, the real estate office sent men around to paint the house, replace broken floor tiles and put in a new stove and refrigerator. And the Bon Visos moved in.

It would take Pete fourteen months to complete the renovation, which cost more than $7,000. Throughout that fall and winter, Paul dropped in every second or third day between tours to help; Pete worked nearly every day. The bedroom and upstairs bathroom had to be framed out with sheetrock. And since there was no heat upstairs, he had to stop long enough to seal the top of the stairs with a trap door.

He was helped occasionally by Buddy, a muscular bull of a man from across the street who came into both cops' lives the day Pete moved in. Buddy worked as an airline fuel distributor, and he saw his new neighbors first when a crowded car had arrived with several friends and both mothers-in-law—and he was horrified, thinking that "a bunch of Puerto Ricans" had moved into the neighborhood. But on moving day, he dropped in for a closer look and spent most of the day moving furniture and boxes.

A solid friendship was formed. Buddy became Pete's and Paul's suburban third man. He began to look like them. Clean-shaven at first, he grew a mustache. Massive at 240 pounds, he dropped to 200. Most important, he joined Pete's construction crew. He was eager to learn the fundamentals of wall and tile work; and since he knew the skills of plumbing and heating, he was a welcome addition.

Pete soon finished the bedroom. At the top of the stairs in front of it he hung a poster-painting of a naked man carrying a naked, submissive woman over the threshold. Then he and Helen moved upstairs.

The den remained. Pete planned it both for children and adults: room for toys, a corner for the bar Rose and Bill had given them, a wall for his wine rack and dart board.

He'd long admired people who kept wine at home. He built two racks, bracing each against the wall and hanging it from the ceiling with a decorative chain. Then he and Helen went shopping, picking wines randomly, choosing as fancy dictated. And thereafter, Pete kept a wine list, carefully noting everything in stock, from Lancers to Liebfraumilch, Champagne to Ruby Port. He had 44 spots to fill. He filled some with better grades of moderately priced Italian wines (he did not feel comfortable in French restaurants, so he was suspicious of French wines) while stocking other spaces with impulsive choices—Jose Hernandez Spanish Red, for example.

He decided the latter was made in dirty bathtubs. "I crossed that right off my fuckin' list," he remembers vehemently.

As he'd hoped, the list was impressive to his guests.

"When we had company, I'd say what kinda wine would you like? And before I said it I'd whip out my little list and let 'em look at it, and I'd take them over to the racks and let them pick out the bottle themselves."

And as his guests selected the evening's wine, Pete glowed like a proud father. "I felt that my house was more complete than anyone else's. I had my own wine selection, even."

The back room was his major showpiece; he completed it by Christmas of 1973. By that time he'd also poured a concrete patio in back, put rain gutters on the roof and extended the breezeway 14 feet so that he could go from the house to garage without stepping outside.

It was a marvelous home—a mirror of Pete Bon Viso's cherished hopes. He had a lovely, happy wife, and soon he would have a son. He was proud. He had every reason to be. All that remained was the upstairs bathroom, and he had no reason to assume he wouldn't finish it.

The young cops' lives became even more intertwined. By now, they were assigned to the same shift, which meant they could ride into work together. At night, they puttered around Pete's house, while the wives stayed in the kitchen. Some evenings Catherine simply stayed home. Carpentry was a male preserve; it was no social evening for her. And by now, Pete and Paul had established a regular pattern of staying overnight at Rose's apartment between back-to-back tours.

The overnights were easy to justify. A night-shift cop who makes an arrest is often required to be in court with the defendant at 8 A.M. That leaves the cop less than eight hours to change out of his uniform, drive home, sleep and return. Living in the city, Pete could do this easily; but commuting back and forth to Copiague (he explained to Helen) exhausted him. And Paul managed to convince Catherine that he had to be with Pete.

On the nights they drove home, they had their code words.

"See you in the morning," meant they would stay away from each other that evening.

"See you later," meant one man would call the other on the military field phone suggesting a movie, drinks or simply getting together.

Dropping Paul, Pete would drive down four houses and walk inside expectantly. *Whatever* had passed between them, the batphone rang within seconds, the first of many calls. One man might call before the other reached home. The field phone was strung from Pete's bathroom window through a neighbor's trees and along a fence running behind two neighboring houses to a tree in Paul's yard, then into Paul's utility room.

In the mornings, one man always called the other after waking up: "just in case the other guy's alarm didn't go off." If Pete was driving, he'd ring Paul again as he left the house. If there was a delay—"if I wanted to take a shower or whatever"—the driver called the other man to advise him.

So the phone rang constantly. Its bell rang flat and low and did not separate into specific signals. The caller simply cranked on one end, and the other end rang until someone picked up. It had an insistent sound, which quickly irritated Catherine.

Already, she resented the intensity of the relationship between Pete and Paul and she began to complain now about the excessive time they spent on the phone. The complaints led only to practical jokes. Driving home, the men planned batphone calls for dramatic effect—a call at precisely 6:15, after Paul had set the stage during dinner.

"Gee, I haven't heard from Paul for a while," he'd say at 14 minutes past the hour.

And the phone would ring.

Catherine was only one victim. In practice, the pranks were fired off like random rock-salt volleys at anyone who came within range.

At Godeffroy during their first summer together as cops, Pete and Paul played a game where one man shot arrows into the air while the other reached for them. The wives, in chorus, objected—a silly, dangerous game, they insisted. So the following day Pete and Paul fired a few desultory rounds until Catherine and Helen went into the house. Then Pete screamed in agony and ran shrieking past the house with an arrow sticking in his chest and fell into the river. Helen and Catherine were deeply frightened—and not amused when he emerged from the water laughing like the village idiot holding the arrow and a styrofoam plate.

Sometimes they ran away from their wives and hid in the woods.

They had a common taste for crude, boyish or overripe humor. The target didn't matter. Many of the jokes were self-inflicted wounds. No subject was taboo: sex, body odor, emotional problems, bad breath, family relations, intellect or lack thereof. It was all a giant, rib-cracking, often savage, long-run joke.

In a health club where they worked out regularly, Paul called an attendant one day to complain that Pete (a supposed stranger) had urinated in his shower stall. The attendant was an obvious homosexual, which heightened the humor; he marched resolutely to Pete's stall. Caught by surprise, Pete was briefly speechless. Then he gaffawed loudly at the wide-eyed attendant, who retreated in confusion.

Buddy, the trusting neighbor, was the easiest mark of all. On hunting trips, the two cops played cowboy, emptying their service revolvers and stalking each other through the woods.

"Stick 'em up!" Pete would yell, sneaking around a tree. They'd slap leather and dry-fire at each other like twin John Waynes.

Buddy, a member of the National Rifle Association, objected vehemently. "You guys are gonna get hurt," he warned again and again.

So for nearly a year, Pete and Paul planned Buddy's comeuppance.

"We primed him even when we weren't hunting," Pete remembered later with a serpent's smile. "In the neighborhood, for example, I kept my gun in the house. But if I was going to work and had to stop at Paul's on the way, I'd have it on. So when Buddy was there, we made a point of dry-firing at each other."

And Buddy always protested.

The following summer, Buddy was at Pete's house. Paul arrived enroute to work, and after a studied pause, the cops started a minor argument which heated up rapidly.

"We'll settle it by drawing," Pete fumed, walking inside for his .38.

Normally, they double-checked the weapons. Today, Pete balked. "It's okay," he said impatiently. "I tell you it's okay." They faced each other.

A small explosion split the warm morning air. Paul clutched at his chest in surprise and pain and fell to the ground.

"Oh my God!" Buddy yelled. He turned pale, staring cow-eyed at Paul who lay motionless on the grass. "Call an ambulance—call the police!"

Pete appeared to be equally frightened, bolting inside for

the telephone, taking the .38 as Buddy danced around Paul's body in panic.

Paul began to shake silently in laughter; and as he did, Buddy's pale fear turned to crimson rage. He bellowed furiously now as Paul—and Pete, returning—fell into convulsions of laughter.

Humor was both a bond and a strange weapon for them; a blade cutting in every direction, sometimes inward. Early in their relationship, Paul discovered that Pete was "easy." Pete played pranks, but he was a far better victim: his fears and insecurities were blatant, like a neon badge. He seemed to hear things. He joked that even huddled football players talked about him. On foot patrol, he often sensed that he was being watched, from a window, perhaps from a distant door. A ringing telephone, he joked endlessly, was for him. At first Paul thought it was all a "goof." But he began to wonder.

Pete, in turn, found that Paul talked of dreams and ambitions, even planned them impulsively—but rarely followed through. It irritated Pete. Paul was trying to impress people falsely, he decided. So he began to pick at this, challenging each suggestion with such force that Paul soon began to feel obliged to follow through even the frailest daydream.

Paul boasted one day at Cal's that he planned to attend Richard Nixon's 1973 inauguration. Pete challenged him. Paul insisted it was no idle boast. For weeks, Pete asked Paul each day if he and Catherine had made reservations for the January 6th spectacle.

Which hotel? And did Paul think his battered car— such a piece of shit!—would survive the trip? Had he taken it in for servicing? Did he have a baby sitter? Had the sergeant given him time off? Was he packed? And on and on.

"Each day I'd remind him," Pete remembers happily, "just to let him know that if he didn't go, he was a piece of shit. And why'd he open his fuckin' mouth in the first place!"

Paul hired a sitter, fixed his car and drove to Washington January 5th with Catherine, staying overnight in a motel. He returned the following day and announced proudly that the mission was accomplished.

"You went to the Bronx and stayed in your relatives' house," grumped Pete.

Paul produced Washington, D.C. match books and cocktail napkins. Pete demanded to check the car's odometer, after which he charged half-seriously that Paul had put the car on a lift and run the wheels.

They carried this and other jokes to limits that defied rational analysis. It was one reason why, for the longest time, Paul saw Victorio Sanchez's reappearance as an equally well-planned, carefully thought-out, insistent . . . prank.

CHAPTER 9

ARGE RILEY had no thought of getting involved with a married man. Blonde and very Irish, iron-willed and thirty, she was a divorcee with two children and strong if informal Catholic values. She would not have gone out with anyone's husband if she'd known.

Pete wore no wedding ring. And in the third year of his marriage, now that he'd begun to look for more than drink and manly conversation on his nights in town, he seemed quite single indeed.

They met on a crowded Friday night in Gleason's, an East Side singles bar. Pete had been pushing his way through a congestion of densely packed drinkers to get relief at the bar when a blonde turned and said huffily:

"I *think* we should get married first."

He blushed briefly, realizing he had worked too hard, an elbow here, a hipbone there. Then he recovered and they began to talk.

Pete soon judged that his unruly behavior was forgotten. He eventually asked if she'd care to accompany him to Thursday's, a bar he felt would be less crowded (and where he knew the maitre d'). Marge said yes.

The maitre d' greeted Pete by name and found them a good table. Pete asked her to dance. But first would she mind keeping something in her purse?

He handed her his gun.

She stopped still. "Are you a cop?"

"Yeah, you got anything against cops?"

"No, my brother-in-law is a cop."

"Okay, let's dance."

She didn't tell him that her ex-husband's friends also carried guns. And that they weren't policemen. And that Pete had looked more to her like one of them than a cop; and that if he were one of them, she wouldn't have agreed to carry his gun.

Still, the evening went well. Pete asked now if she'd like to go to a "friend's apartment." They'd have a few more drinks.

"If you've got tricks up your sleeve, forget it."

"No, no. None of that kinda stuff at all."

It was a lie; and an introduction to the more complex side of Pete Bon Viso. The apartment belonged to a man whose work required constant traveling. He was convinced that a cop's periodic visits would discourage burglars, so he let Pete use it as a pied-a-terre: expensive furniture, original prints on the walls, exotic knickknacks.

It was one of Pete's *secret* places. Pete had other hiding places—apartments and back street social clubs which allowed him to live apart from himself, as if he had two identities; or more. He loved having secret places in his life. His motives weren't always sexual; just as often, they were conspiratorial. *His* conspiracy.

And so Marge Riley arrived at the secret midtown apartment. She sat next to Pete on an expensive couch with a huge rubber tree beside it, and she talked with this man who promised no tricks.

At 2 A.M. it seemed time to go home.

He said no. He wanted her to stay the night.

He sat sullenly next to the rubber tree plant holding his drink as she left. She hailed a taxi and assumed she wouldn't see him again.

Pete called to apologize the morning after. Marge accepted this, but said she had no interest in dating him. He called again. He called several times a day "just to talk." That Valentine's Day he sent an unsigned orchid. She called the florist and confirmed her suspicions, but she still tried to resist him. Then he asked if he could drive her home after work. She let him. He began asking for dates and demanding explanations when she said no, which she always did. One night he demanded that she break a date in order to see him; she refused.

"Make sure you don't go to any cheap motels," he sneered into the phone.

She slammed it down. He called back to apologize.

Two months later, the affair finally began. He doubled

the telephone calls, checking in four, five, six times a day, whenever he happened to be near a telephone. They were together three, sometimes four nights a week while he was working on Avenue C, commuting back and forth to Long Island, maintaining what seemed a placid marriage, rebuilding his house, accompanying Helen to a doctor in the hope of starting a family.

In that context, Marge was perfect for him. She didn't wish to see Pete all the time, anyway. She preferred to be alone. She was a short, chunky woman with frosted hair and blue eyes—a hint of freckles about her nose, on her hands—and her manner had both a hard edge and an oddly beguiling warmth to it. She'd had a full share of difficulty: troubled teen-age years followed by a bad marriage to a sometime mobster named Vince (who called her Maisie and was still around), and she wanted time now for herself, her children, her job. She wanted no full-time relationship.

Besides, the affair was less than rosy. In its first two years, Pete and Marge broke up more than 30 times by her count. But Pete's persistence, sometimes bordering on lunacy, always patched things up. Marge ended it the first time when she found out he was twenty-four years old. He'd told her he was thirty-five.

The next separation occurred when she learned that he was married.

"You are a low-class individual!" she screamed at him. Pete pleaded that he hadn't wanted to lose her. He called day after day and sent flowers. He waited outside her apartment, begging, pleading.

"I won't stay away!" he wailed each time. "You can't

keep me away. I'll stand by your door. I'll be outside your job. I'll be on the phone." In the end, she let him have his way.

As if to balance it, she gave no ground in other areas. She shared an apartment with her mother and she made it clear that it was no home for him. She also insisted that her life be independent. She would not be attached to him in any formal way, she said.

As a result, Pete wanted her desperately. She was no pushover like so many women on Avenue C who assumed that a uniform just naturally contained an impressive man. She forced him to use his fullest bag of tricks: slavish devotion, passionate declarations, exotic gifts—followed by manipulative treatment and lies.

Marge kept cool during the passionate declarations, and she retaliated harshly to bad treatment.

"He was full of lies," she remembers of the early days. "It was lie after lie."

On one occasion when he broke a date in order to go to the race track—and lied about it—she went out with Vince, who was happy to oblige her. Pete became insanely jealous. He started one of his periodic campaigns to become "perfect" for her. He began a diet, bought new clothes, and became cloyingly courtly. He was deeply, angrily jealous of Vince.

"What about Helen?" Marge always answered. He did not see the comparison.

In the beginning of the relationship, he talked little of himself or his feelings. Sometimes he became inexplicably angry, lapsing into dark silence. He could not be coaxed into revealing, even minutely, how she might help him. So she ignored him, which made Pete even angrier. Even when his anger gave way to quiet tears, she ignored him. As it happened, the tears were a sign of progress in their relationship. For eventually, Pete began to talk more freely of himself, which often made him cry. She thought the tears theatrical and did not trust them

She was also perplexed and irritated by his extreme physical dependence on her. When they were together, Pete was a big Italian lap dog. He aggressively involved himself in *all* her conversations; he rarely ventured more than a few feet away, and he returned quickly. She noticed he was this way with Paul, too, and she assumed he behaved similarly with Helen. He seemed to be afraid to be alone.

"Marge," a girlfriend once remarked acidly, "one day he's gonna just grab your face and stick it into his." Marge laughed, but she remembered the remark.

Without him, Marge led a quiet life at her mother's apartment. She watched television, read magazines and spent time with her children. At night she went out to uptempo sociable bars like Gleason's and Little John's with her girlfriends. By day she was the president's secretary in a small publishing house, putting in long hours. Her ex-husband paid the support money irregularly. When he held back, she went to court.

"I've had it very tough," she observed once. "I don't mind now, but there were times when I became very depressed."

Vince happened to see Pete and Marge together one day. He was driving a Cadillac and wearing a custom-tailored silk suit, and Pete, unshaven and sad-eyed, wore dungarees and sneakers. Vince telephoned his ex-mother-in-law in a frenzy.

"Mom," he exploded. "I just seen Maisie coming out of work with some broken-down suitcase. I told you it would come to this! I *told* you she'd end up washing some Guinea's socks." Marge's mother already considered Pete a gambler and a drunk. She told the story gleefully.

But Marge came to believe that Pete truly loved her. She believed finally that he loved her more than any woman in his life. And in those moments, she thought of the good times, when he was gentle and good with her, when he seemed more devoted than any man she'd known. And as a result, she returned his love. She loved him during the best and worst of times. There were plenty of both.

CHAPTER 10

IN late June, he saw Sanchez a third time. Again, Paul was not with him when it happened.

The two cops had been walking along Eighth Street checking buildings, and Paul wanted to use a toilet. They walked toward the avenue, and Paul disappeared into a social club while Pete stood outside.

He saw Sanchez across the avenue, alone.

No mistake. It *was* Sanchez. Absolutely still, the gunman stared fiercely at him, mouthing a mute challenge across the space between them. For a moment Pete could hardly believe his opponent's boldness. Sanchez had to be a fugitive, yet he seemed unconcerned about his safety. He wasn't afraid of Pete; he seemed to be unarmed. Pete could take away his freedom—did he realize that?

But Sanchez seemed to know that the young cop would do nothing more than look back at him. Pete saw that the gunman wore familiar black clothing, hands draped down in his gunfighter's pose. Sanchez's silence, even across a noisy avenue, was deafening.

The gunman turned and walked around the corner, disappearing. Pete rushed across Avenue C. He saw nothing.

"That's it," he muttered. "That motherfucker is *out.*"

Paul walked out of the social club, straightening himself. Pete turned to him anxiously. "You finished?" he asked.

"Yes." Paul looked at his partner curiously. "Why?"

"Because Sanchez is out. I just saw him."

"You kidding?" But Paul looked at his friend and knew that something was wrong.

"I don't know how he's out," Pete continued, talking rapidly. "Maybe he's on good behavior—maybe he escaped. But he's out! I just saw him go up Eighth Street. Let's go! Let's check it out."

Paul drew back. He knew that Pete had an exceptional memory for faces. "You sure?"

"Positive."

They walked down the grim and littered sidestreet, checking hallways and vacant buildings, watching every face.

"You *sure?*"

Pete became annoyed. "Paul," he said slowly, angrily, "I know what I saw." He nodded his head as he talked, as if to agree with himself.

They returned to the avenue. For the moment there was nothing to do. Paul thought of calling the District Attorney's office. Pete usually did this kind of thing, since he was more adept at dealing with the bureaucracy, but this time

Paul volunteered. And as they talked, Paul wondered about his partner. Was this some kind of joke? It made no sense that Sanchez should be back on the street.

Had Pete begun an elaborate prank? It's possible, he thought. It was always possible. They were so close now that pranks could safely violate even the most sacred trusts. Reality had a recurring flip-side in their relationship. For a variety of reasons, Paul resolved to check on Sanchez. He believed—at least in part—that the fear he saw in his friend's eyes was real. He had seen it before.

But he also know that when Pete established a particular fear's validity, he might decide to use it as a weapon—anything for a laugh. They'd planned the joke on Buddy for a long, long time. Paul resolved to keep his guard up.

He would not be fooled by some crazy prank.

And for more than six months of Pete's terror, he would cling to the belief that it *was* a prank.

When they quarreled, something in Pete slammed shut. Whatever Paul had said or done to upset him—now the fights often involved Paul's ambivalence about Sanchez—was not immediately revealed. For it was not Pete's way to react visibly to an insult or to annoyance. He became silent, and when his silence became obvious, Paul still had to figure out its cause. This led to yet another impasse, since Paul, a proud man, rarely admitted *his* complicity in a quarrel.

Pete might spread his silence over several days, like a shroud. Only when the air had become so heavy that Pete felt his friend had suffered enough would he talk.

They had predictable ignition points. Paul's "plans" upset

Pete, leading to such feuds as the Nixon Inaugural incident. Another quarrel occurred whenever (always at the last minute, Pete charged) Paul and Catherine failed to find a babysitter after being invited to dinner. Pete felt it an affront to his abilities as a host, or a sign that Paul didn't really like him—or worse, that Catherine, who was cool to him anyway, had managed to sabotage yet another of their evenings together.

Quarrels disrupted their lives like a constantly-late commuter train. And when they did, silence reigned on Avenue C. Pete might stalk the street in a deathmask for hours.

"When I'm angry," Pete explained once, "I act like I don't wanta talk about it, but deep down, I do. But until the person asks me about it, I try to make his life miserable. If he asks me once, I'll make him ask me a couple more times until I get to a point where I say all right—*now* I'll tell you why I'm making your life miserable. Paul knew me pretty well, of course. And he knew the best way to break my balls was to let me stew."

By contrast, Paul's anger came fast. If something upset him, his boyish face fell into darkness—words and actions followed like lethal rain. And just as suddenly, it was over.

But since open anger was not Bill Bon Viso's way of dealing with a hostile world, it would not be Pete's. On the Avenue, Paul nearly always used his club first. Pete surpassed him only once, and it took an odd insult to bring out Pete's supressed violence—one against his father.

They'd passed Seventh Street just after the dinner hour, and half a dozen young Puerto Ricans stood outside a liquor store drinking from a bottle of cheap Port. New York City law prohibits passing a "common bottle" outdoors, but Pete and Paul rarely bothered anyone who did. If anything, they might tell the drinkers to put the bottle away while they passed, to show "respect."

This time Pete heard someone say something, followed by the words "your father . . ."

He doesn't remember how he hit the kid. He remembers that he turned hot and felt his ears burning, and he remembers turning his body and seeing the flat of his hand come around, as if it belonged to someone else. The kid was short and thin and about 19, and Pete knocked him to the ground. Then he began to kick him. Paul joined in. They grabbed the kid and threw him against a parked car.

"You wanta repeat what you said?" Pete growled menacingly.

"No, man, I didn't say nuthin'—I wasn't talkin' to you." The kid couldn't seem to believe what was happening to him.

Pete stared at him briefly, cursed and reached for the bottle. He broke it against the curb.

"Now get the fuck outta here!" The kid and his friends moved out quickly. Afterward, Pete wondered if the kid was from his old neighborhood; he hadn't recognized the face. Had the kid ever *seen* his father? He thought about the incident for a long time.

"I've got you," Paul grinned.

They were driving on the Long Island Expressway. Paul was at the wheel. They'd been drinking wine, and the talk had no particular direction. Before Paul spoke, the car had been silent.

"What?" Pete was lost in another dream.

"The guy's in jail."

"Bullshit!" Pete was into it now, fast. "I know he's *not* in jail."

"Yeah? I called up the D.A. who handled the case. He's in jail."

"Then he paid somebody to be in jail for him. I've seen him too many times to be wrong."

Paul looked at his partner. That was a *weird* thing to say. It had to be a joke, a "supergoof." And he knew it would be the long, extended kind.

"All right," he laughed bravely, "lay off, okay? He's in jail. I know it; you know it."

But now he saw the sad face he associated with Pete's worst crises, when Pete's fingers dawdled beside a slack mouth, when his silence was utterly dark.

Paul watched the traffic around him and considered his options. Pete was bringing up the heavy artillery, he decided. He was pushing. At first, Paul had believed the story. On the avenue that day, he'd thought, shit, that fucking guy is out already? He was supposed to get two to five. What happened? Shortly after that, he'd bumped into Luis Navarro, the timid witness.

"Heads up," he warned. "Blackie's out."

Then he'd called Jerry McNulty, the assistant district attorney who prosecuted the case. McNulty had assured him the gunman was safely tucked away.

Changing lanes, Paul decided that Pete was being a poor sport. He put it out of his mind and brought up another subject.

They didn't talk about Sanchez again for weeks.

Catherine Rossi was extremely upset. She had read a magazine article about the pop-sociological phenomenon of police partnerships "more intimate than marriage." She was particularly disturbed by the article's profile of a team nicknamed Batman and Robin who reminded her of Pete and Paul. For it was clear that such partners were more loyal to each other than to their wives, reserving their innermost feelings for each other. They had a separate consciousness, sometimes separate lives; and no wife could intrude.

She was briefly fascinated; then horrified. As it happened, she did not find the company of cops particularly satisfying at any time. She often remembered an evening spent among Paul's Ninth Precinct friends in his rookie days. The cops drank heavily, cracked crude jokes and played a "dirty" record. At Paul's request, she'd brought a girlfriend to the party, another nurse, for an informal pairing with a single cop. But the night was unspeakably raw; she was embarrassed for weeks afterward. She and Paul and the girlfriend rode back to Long Island in silence.

Her experiences with Pete sustained that bad memory. As she saw it, her husband and his friend had regressed to a vulgar childhood she neither liked nor understood. Pete often appeared at her house without Helen. They sat in the living room drinking wine, talking shop and making tasteless jokes, excluding her. She went to bed early those nights, but sometimes she only pretended to retire, sitting at the top of the stairs, listening. What in God's name could they be sharing? She never heard anything worth passing on.

It was the intimacy which bothered her. Paul's deepest feelings—ecstacy, love, pain—should be shared with her. They were of one flesh; *she* had cleaved to him and given him children. She deeply resented Pete's encroachments on this. Her marriage was foundering, and the wedge between them, the symbol of it all, was Pete Bon Viso.

It was no easy thing to fight.

She showed the article to them. And she was further humiliated. For she somehow assumed that Pete and Paul would see the eccentricity of their behavior—and the damage it was doing to her—and would change.

But Pete and Paul ignored her anger completely. They loved the article; they talked endlessly of it, comparing themselves proudly to the cops they read about, basking in the reflected glory of it. Catherine became even more angry.

She managed one major victory during this period. She and Paul moved off the block.

It happened that they were already restless in their Copiague house, which was showing its age and had become too small for their growing family. Most important, they'd long dreamed of living in a semi-rural setting near woods and water. And one winter afternoon, she chanced upon an oddly seductive newspaper advertisement. A picture showed trees and a vast expanse of ocean.

"Panoramic Harbor View—Oldie but Goodie House,' the copy read. The picture seemed almost alive. She showed it to Paul, who agreed to see it. It started a round of serious house-hunting, a bond which Pete couldn't share.

Eventually, they decided to buy a lot and build rather

than take over a dream slipping away from someone else. Paul's brother agreed to help, and they settled on a wooded half-acre in Port Jefferson, a town more than 50 miles (and 90 minutes driving time) from Manhattan. They constructed a warm, pleasant, suburban-style house with a spacious living room and picture windows looking out at the trees. In summer and fall, when everything bloomed, they couldn't see their neighbors, and they liked this.

To no one's surprise, Pete was not pleased. He muttered about the project's "outta sight cost," and he told friends that Paul had made a terrible mistake, going heavily into debt, taking on a long commute. The grounding of the batphone wire was the saddest moment of all. It was also the most symbolic. Catherine now had reason to hope that Paul would talk to *her*. No one spoke of it, but the move was also an attempt to save their marriage.

But the partnership continued to flourish. Pete and Paul considered themselves the toast of Avenue C, a police team without peer: tight, ready for action. They worked hard. In countless nights on the job, they planned and discussed every emergency situation they could think of. The idea was to be able to move without talking; to know instinctively what the other man would do. They rehearsed imaginary scenes: stopping cars, burglaries-in-progress, robberies, who went in the front door, who covered the back, who radioed for back-up. They rehearsed street confrontations so they might approach and disarm a suspicious man flawlessly.

They memorized addresses. An emergency call might bring news of a burglary-in-progress at 318 East Eighth

Street, apartment 5. It was their business to know that 318 was a five-story tenement, that apartment 5 was in the back, that the building had a fire escape on its south side, that the building's back door led to an alley.

Stopping cars required equally precise teamwork. Early in the partnership, they had stopped a car circling a block host to a great deal of heroin traffic—then lost it when the car lurched away after they'd left their own. They'd tried to chase the fleeing car, but it was no use. The patrol car was a typical six-cylinder slug ravished by years of department use, and the opposition flew away in a Pontiac Grand Prix. But they'd learned something. After that, Pete and Paul radioed their location and the suspect car's color and direction before they got out.

On court nights they stayed with Rose regularly now. They started these nights with a drink at Cal's, followed by a visit to Jack LaLanne's Health Spa for pingpong and weight-lifting. They played pingpong to see who would pay for dinner; Pete usually lost. Afterward, they plunged into a whirlpool bath, where Paul invariably talked of the expensive food he planned to order.

In the bars and restaurants, Pete spent money without flinching, buying drinks and dinners as if he'd just gotten a raise. He wore colorful open-necked shirts, sharply creased pants and kept his hair fashionably styled. If it was Pete's poker night, they went to his game together. Paul sometimes put in money and acted as Pete's conscience. He stood behind his friend, watched the cards and tried to pull Pete out when Pete's natural aggressiveness was pulling them under. Sometimes Paul put up half of Pete's stake—

not an easy thing to do. For Pete might throw $50 into the pot on impossible odds. And when he did, Paul cursed under his breath, wishing he could yank his $25 *out,* all the while remaining deadpan so as to give nothing away.

If they didn't gamble, they drank. They went to Gleason's, Thursday's, Little John's, the Gloccomora, an East Side bar frequented by cops. They played the games that men play during a night on the town, strutting, hanging out, talking that talk, cruising from place to place. Sometimes Pete brought Marge along. And eventually, they'd begin to move in a roundabout, drunken way toward the Lower East Side.

Each night, Rose waited for them. She fixed a late meal if they wanted it; she made breakfast in the morning, hovering, hanging on their words, inserting her opinions about family matters.

She accepted, too, the duty of rousting them from drugged slumber after a raucous night. One man usually staggered out first, and she joined forces with him against the other. The late sleeper was then victimized by cold water, tickling, loud noises—occasionally something more. Pete, for example, pushed his feet out of the covers as he slept. Paul inserted a wooden match between two of his toes one morning, nestling the head between the pig who went to market and the pig who stayed home. He lit the wooden end, and he and Rose settled back to watch it burn.

Pete clawed his way out of darkness in explosive pain. He lurched forward and saw his mother and his best friend convulsed in laughter. And when he realized what had happened, he yowled like a dog, threatening violence as they ran to the kitchen where a teapot whistled. "You better sleep with one eye open," he warned Paul over the morning tea. But he did nothing. He was a better victim than terrorist.

CHAPTER 11

Pᴀᴜʟ had Air National Guard duty that Saturday in 1973; and so Pete drove home alone, speeding as recklessly as always, cutting in and out of traffic as though the other cars hardly existed, puffing away at his cigar, humming to the blaring radio.

Just out of the city, he noticed an old Chevrolet in his rear-view mirror. It was extremely old, maybe 1956, painted bright yellow. He watched it with idle curiosity. Haven't seen a '56 Chevy in *years,* he thought. In the sideview mirror now, he watched the car move into the passing lane. He didn't particularly like to be passed, so he glanced more than casually at the driver.

He was astonished to see Victorio Sanchez! Pete nearly swallowed his cigar.

Jesus! This wasn't Avenue C, it was the Northern State

Parkway! Christ, he was going home where he was supposed
to be safe! The bastard was tailing him.

Pete stomped on his brake pedal, skidded onto the grassy
embankment. He jumped out and scurried behind the car.
What the fuck was going *on?* He reached for his off-duty
gun and braced it with two hands on the hood of the car.
He crouched behind the car like a soldier in a foxhole,
rotating his head slowly back and forth scanning the road,
his small cannon pointed squarely at the traffic.

But Sanchez was gone. The traffic had moved on without
noticing him, or his gun; he saw no yellow Chevrolet. He
saw nothing, just the blur of passing cars. He heard nothing, only the traffic and his own breathing. He put the gun
away, still kneeling.

Easy now. Pete watched the parkway a minute longer.
Then he secured his gun and stood up. He walked around
to the driver's side of the car, looked one more time and
got in.

Pete fell in with the traffic and headed again for home,
thinking about what had happened. That motherfucker!
Now I gotta start carrying a shotgun in the car. This is
bad, really bad.

He punched the throttle and moved in and out of traffic
even more recklessly, watching both mirrors. The yellow
Chevrolet had to be ahead of him. So far, nothing. He
drove faster.

Sanchez was beside him like a night rider. The yellow
Chevrolet pushed close, crossing almost into Pete's lane.
Pete could see the heat in his enemy's face. The car pushed
even closer. Sanchez was trying to run him off the road!
That sonofabitch! That bastard!

Pete worked his gun free. He and Sanchez screamed silently at each other through the car windows and faced each other nearly door to door as the cars rushed forward. Pete raised his pistol. I'll blast that sonofabitch out of the road! He steadied the gun in the window and aimed it directly at the gunman's hateful eyes.

Sanchez roared away, leaving Pete in his exhaust as if the Chevy had a racing engine. For a moment Pete just stared after him in shock. Now he careened off an exit ramp on screaming tires. He raced through stoplights and across intersections in several small towns until he was certain no one followed him; then he doubled back, approaching Copiague by a back route.

He couldn't let Sanchez find his house!

He raced down the block now and pulled into his driveway with squealing tires, jumping out, running through the front door, past Helen without a word, up the stairs. Working feverishly, he loaded his guns and leaned them against the bed, finishing as Helen approached him.

"Pete?"

He said nothing.

"Pete, what's the matter?"

"Nuthin'." He avoided her eyes.

"Pete, what are these guns all about?"

"Look, I hadda rough day at the job. Leave me alone, okay? What's for dinner?"

He hadn't told her anything about Sanchez. He'd told no one except Paul. As always, he refused to bring his troubles home—though in Sanchez's case it was beginning to look like he had no choice. Still, he put off telling her. During a morose and silent dinner, he mentioned vaguely that someone tried to force him off the highway coming home. He offered no details; typically, she asked for none. Helen rarely questioned Pete. She was grateful that he existed, that they had a home, that they were married, that a child was coming. She was heavy with her pregnancy now, well into her sixth month. Whenever Pete kept things from her, which he did often, she fell back on the assumption that he'd had "hassles" as a child. She routinely accepted Pete's silence. He insisted that some things couldn't be talked about; and she believed him.

But tonight she boiled with questions.

After dinner as they watched television, Pete kept a fully loaded gun within arm's reach. Beside it, he remained ominously silent, as if disaster was about to strike. She grew extremely uncomfortable.

"Why are you keeping the gun so close?" she finally asked.

"I like the gun."

Again he avoided her eyes. But he caught himself and smiled briefly. "You remember when I was a rookie, I usta keep it around all the time? I just feel like keeping it around again." He turned to the TV again.

But until recently, he'd kept it in a closed drawer. He kept it there unless he had to go out, or to work—plus or minus an occasional quick-draw contest. So Helen sat on the couch in her maternity clothing, pregnant with questions. But she didn't bring it up again.

The following day, he told Paul.

"What?" Paul was stunned. Was Pete *still* pushing this

thing? "Are you kidding?" he asked impatiently. "I told you the guy's in jail."

"Paul, I wouldn't make something like this up," Pete answered evenly. He was deeply angry that Paul didn't believe him.

This prank, Paul decided, was a pain. How long before Pete pulled the string? Maybe Helen would call him on the weekend—she had to be in on it, too—and tell him that Pete had barricaded the house! It was ridiculous.

He began looking for a way to head it off.

That day on the Bowery, Paul noticed a black beadwork medallion among some trinkets outside a novelty shop. It was a round medallion with a good luck symbol of white beads at its center. It was the sort of cheap trinket tourists bought as Indian jewelry. It could be worn as a necklace.

Paul paid fifty cents for it.

"This'll protect you from Sanchez when I'm not around," he told Pete the next day, suppressing a laugh. If Pete wanted to keep this dumb gag going, he'd be forced to wear this ridiculous thing. And he'd have to keep wearing it until he gave up.

Advantage Rossi. Or so he thought.

But Pete was delighted with the gift. He was so pleased that Paul at last believed him that he began wearing the medallion *over* his uniform. A sergeant noticed it one night and ordered him to take it off and Pete refused, joking that it had religious meaning. He looked after the medallion as if it were gold. He cradled it softly in his hands, suspended it delicately in the locker when he changed clothes, displayed it proudly.

For a while, Paul was completely thrown by this. Why

was Pete pushing so hard? It was crazy to be pushing a joke so compulsively. Briefly, he wondered if Pete had, well . . . a screw loose. But that made no sense. His partner's behavior in every other way seemed perfectly normal— obnoxious sometimes, odd and unpredictable, but always within reasonable boundaries. Yet this obsession was becoming a pain in the ass.

For a long time, pranks and craziness aside, they'd done well on the avenue. Among Ninth Precinct Neighborhood Police Teams, they ranked third and fourth in arrests. If they happened to be on 14th Street when the radio alerted them to trouble on 4th, they happily ran to it. They wanted to be first; they wanted the arrest. They began each day early and left the streets at the last possible moment, covering the avenue as if it belonged to them. They felt they were giving what cops call "nine hours in eight"— hustling, running around, moving.

They felt ready, in fact, for glamour, and they asked to be assigned to the anti-crime patrol, the crime busters. The anti-crime squads were new to the department, and the men in them enjoyed considerable prestige: television spots, magazine articles, newspaper pictures of cops disguised as Santa Claus at Christmas time. The squads worked high-crime areas in street disguises, interrupting stick-ups, muggings and other mayhem in progress. It was an action job. They felt they were ready for it.

The summer of 1973, in fact, the squad had met and voted Pete and Paul in, unofficially. Jerry Bono, already a member, lobbied hard for them.

But the squad was overruled. The transfer had to come

from the precinct's high command—and one sergeant remembered a night two years earlier when Pete and Paul had disappeared and gone to sleep—"cooping," in police slang—during a midnight tour. He argued it would be even easier for them to disappear in plain clothes; besides, he didn't trust them.

Pete and Paul became redfaced and furious. They'd thought the incident was forgotten. They reacted as if they'd been kicked. It wasn't fair!

One slipup so long ago! The bosses forget what it's like to be in the streets. And besides, they'd changed. They were hauling ass now. They were gung-ho cops. Look what it had gotten them . . .

They complained loudly to the sergeant who ran the Neighborhood Police Teams. He commiserated. Go back to the avenue, he said. Be patient. I'll see what I can do.

And like kids being dragged out of the movies, they returned. They cursed and grumbled, and for a while, they kept the dream alive. For more than a month, they worked hard; they moved fast.

But by August their pride wilted in the late summer's heat. They cursed their bureaucratic fate and came to bitterness. They felt they'd been stepped on, rejected. They became defiant. They began to slow down: *screw* the department. Trouble ten blocks away provoked only indifference; they walked to it. On other days, they hung out idly, talking to Abie, or Sam the candy man, or other local favorites. On rainy days, they stayed inside. They took long "personals" and longer lunch hours. They saw no reason for spit-shined shoes and sharply pressed uniforms. And they were late to work as often as they came on time.

Most of all, they lost interest in "catching." Pete and Paul stopped bothering the junkies on Ninth Street, and they gave up the investigations which sometimes led them to burglars and drug dealers. They made only the easiest arrests. By late August, they'd dropped from third and fourth in arrests to eighteenth and nineteenth among neighborhood police teams.

In cop language, they "died."

And retribution was swift. The sergeant who'd earlier counseled patience became an angry bureaucrat. If they weren't "catching," he wanted parking tickets, which they hated to give.

"What *is* this?" the sergeant demanded. They had no answer. "So at least give me summonses," he said. "You gotta be showing something for your time." They gave him nothing.

He threatened to break them up, and they scoffed at the idea, thinking they were inviolate. The avenue would go crazy without us, they boasted.

They were separated and thrown out of the neighborhood police teams in mid-September—one week before Pete saw Sanchez on the Grand Central Parkway.

Paul was assigned day work while Pete remained on four-to-twelves. Pete was badly upset. Now he couldn't ride to work with Paul; and since Paul no longer lived in Copiague, the change cut deeply into their off-duty time. He couldn't understand it. He felt the department was punishing him unjustly. He raged against the decision. He drank deeply over it at night, complaining bitterly to all who would listen. But there was nothing he could do—and the worst was coming.

He stayed in the city one Tuesday in October after a four-to-midnight tour and drank morosely, sailing into darkness on a boatload of dry Manhattans, waking in the morning with bloodshot eyes, a bad stomach, a thundering headache. Dragging into Cal's for club soda and aspirin, he was accosted by two colleagues.

"Hey, we heard you and your partner got transferred."

"What?" Pete's head throbbed badly.

"We heard you guys got transferred," a third cop added.

"What is this, some kinda joke?" Pete said weakly. "We just got broken up. I don't need this."

But it was true. They were suddenly reassigned to a Fifth Precinct "security detail"—separate jobs patrolling empty hallways in the newly constructed headquarters building near City Hall. Guard duty in an empty building! No more war stories—no street action. Pete's head hurt far worse than when he walked into Cal's. He decided to take a "personal" day off. What the hell, it was his last tour.

But the desk sergeant offered him no sympathy. "I'm short on men," he said quickly. "I need you. Put on your uniform."

"Look at me, I'm a fucking wreck," Pete pleaded. "My eyes are sticking out of my head. I'm sick as a dog."

He signed out and walked back to Cal's to brood. The sergeant followed him. "If you're sick, go home," he growled. "Otherwise, turn out."

"Sarge, gimme a break, wouldja? It's my last day in the precinct."

"Turn out. I need you."

"Like a hole in the head."

And the sergeant stalked back into the precinct house and marked Pete AWOL. It was the beginning of a great deal of trouble.

Each night in the new headquarters building, he grew more restless. No one to talk to. A great job if you hate police work, he thought. He had a desk and a telephone—he could make calls at least—but *nothing* to do. Five cops for each eight-hour shift, two for the VIP entrance, two at the main entrance, one for relief—twenty-four rejects in all to cover a full week's tours. They'd dubbed themselves the "Dirty Dozen."

He'd made new friends, of course. For a while he and the others talked of nothing but how each of them had fallen from grace. The stories fascinated him. One cop had killed two civilians and a dog, but most of the men were amiable mavericks like himself, sent downtown because of absenteeism, lack of polish, chronic tardiness or disputes with their precinct superiors. "Okay, what'd *you* do?" was the standard opening line, and Pete enjoyed the stories for a while.

But he grew increasingly restless. It was a convenient post, several blocks from his mother's apartment. The previous weekend, he'd brought Helen into town for a Saturday wedding, then walked to work that Sunday morning. But he was still a street cop. He loved moving around, talking to people, catching; he was no door guard. *Look* at this, he thought, walking into the building, eyeing it in disgust. Look at this, I'm gonna be sitting around in this big fuckin' dungeon for who knows how long. *I'm gonna go fuckin' crazy in this place.* So far, he and Paul had crossed paths only twice.

He began to wander through the long empty hallways. He and the others made paper airplanes, played pranks, threw spitballs, started games of tag. And he wandered. The building's elevators didn't work, the lights were minimal, so he climbed the stairs and prowled the hallways with his flashlight, angry at what his life had become.

On his first payday on the new job, he climbed to the fourth floor to look at the departmental trial room. In the darkness, his flashlight formed a lone tunnel of light, playing off tables and chairs.

He heard a noise. Behind him, a door closed.

Pete whirled around and saw nothing but darkness. He remembered leaving a hallway door ajar, but when he heard nothing more he assumed that air currents had closed it. He turned his attention again to the trial room, imagining himself on the bench. He walked toward it, focusing the beam idly, lost in a make-believe world. Finally he turned toward the room's door to leave—and froze.

Victorio Sanchez was standing by the door, glaring at him.

The gunman didn't move. He kept his hands in the pockets of a long black coat as if he had his pistol now. Sanchez was framed in darkness: the short muscular body Pete knew all too well, the round face and dark eyes. He stood by the door like a statue of the devil, saying nothing.

Pete's heart exploded, thumping like a drum. He snapped off his flashlight so that Sanchez couldn't make a target of him, and he dropped to the floor. He inched toward the door and saw no one. He ran out of it, flying down the stairs. How did that bastard get in the building!

Downstairs, he composed himself. He couldn't show panic. He didn't want the other cops on the shift to think he was . . . crazy or something. He reached for the medallion inside his shirt.

Gone! He'd left it at home—Paul was right!

His shift partner was sitting at the sentry table, and he relaxed a little. He had help now, extra guns.

"Listen," he said tentatively, "I saw something on the fourth floor."

"What'd you see?"

"Uh . . . I saw the trial room. You ever see the trial room?"

"What?"

"The trial room, you know? You might be going there someday," he joked nervously. "Now's the time to see it for free." Pete worked hard. He couldn't admit he'd seen Sanchez. The gunman might have left, and it would be embarrassing. But if he hadn't, Pete desperately wanted another cop up there. Maybe they could corner Sanchez, run him down, *end this once and for all.*

Pete talked on as the precious seconds passed. Finally, the cop agreed to go upstairs, and they started up, making jokes in the dark, throwing paper airplanes.

The room was empty.

Pete glanced nervously at the door. He watched the dark hallway as the other cop wandered over to the presiding officer's bench. Pete felt better now. He had another gun

now, and Sanchez must have gotten out of the building
the same way he got in, whatever that was.

He relaxed and joined the other man. They wrote ob-
scene messages on the presiding officer's bench and left.

It was November of 1973, during America's worst energy
crisis in decades, and Pete and Paul had been apart for
nearly three months, meeting only when and if their
schedules allowed time for a quick drink or a meal. Pete
missed his partner terribly. Then as winter approached and
there was increasing talk of a fuel shortage, he had an
idea.

"Paul, let's talk to the boss," he said suddenly. "Give him
a little bullshit, tell 'em we'll ride to work together to save
energy. It's patriotic to save energy. We'll appeal to his
patriotism!"

Paul suppressed a laugh. Yet he knew Pete could talk a
fireman out of his hose under the right circumstances.

In a week the Fifth Precinct commander moved Pete
into Paul's squad. They took an extra midnight tour as a
concession, but it was settled. "Pretty" and "Prettier" were
a team again! They might spend whole days together now,
talking, joking, enjoying each other. They could eat a
Steak 'n Brew, visit the bars, play pingpong at Jack La-
Lanne's . . .

So now they made the best of their purgatory, assuming
it would be over in good time. Pete began a beard, and he
let his mustache grow down to a scraggly Fu Manchu.
Paul cultivated longer hair and sideburns. Along with the
rest of the Dirty Dozen, both men lost interest in any sort

of spit and polish appearance. Pete altered his uniform to include levis. And as long as they remained hidden, the bosses didn't seem to mind. They considered The Dozen lepers, keeping them at a distance as if failure were a contagious disease.

Late that month, the department announced an official ribbon-cutting ceremony and moved the Dozen out. Pete and Paul's new assignment was *old* headquarters, an ancient fortress on Centre Street. The building was dark and mostly deserted, bedecked with scaffolding, awaiting a vague future.

When they arrived, the wrecker's ball seemed its most likely future. The old headquarters was now a dead-end building guarded by equally dead-end cops, home to an odd-lot overflow of workers from other law enforcement agencies who didn't fit in elsewhere. A small number of police laboratory technicians worked in the basement, and some of the Special State Prosecutor Maurice Nadjari's investigators had offices near the side corridor that contained the lockers Pete and Paul used.

The building's remaining tenants shuffled through the gloom like ghosts. Rodents and cockroaches, emboldened by the emptiness, scurried around the trash piles. If the bright new headquarters building had seemed a dungeon to Pete, this was a tomb. He let his beard bloom fully. He brought in a dart board and a television set. He watched football games and stayed near a phone so he could call his bookie and everyone else in town, including Marge Riley, three or four times a day.

The days dragged on. They'd assumed the detail would last three months at most. December arrived, the third month. They dropped into Cal's occasionally, but it was depressing to listen to *other* cop's stories. Boredom tightened around them like a noose.

Christmas came. Pete now had one bright spot in his life: the imminent arrival of his first child. A baby was Helen's cherished dream, and after a year of unsuccessful starts and considerable tension, she'd become pregnant the previous spring. The doctor predicted a baby any day.

And Christmas passed. On December 27th, Pete and Paul drove to the old headquarters for a night tour and found that Helen had called while they were on the road. She was in labor. Buddy's wife had taken her to Syosset General Hospital, where the doctors pronounced her labor false. But Pete had a feeling, and he bought champagne, pouring drinks for everyone in the building.

The partners continued celebrating the anticipated good news until the bars closed, arriving at Rose's apartment several hours into the new day.

She waited radiantly with the news—Pete had a son!

In the morning Pete asked for a day off to visit Helen and his son. The desk sergeant was happy to oblige.

"Uh, sarge, my partner drove in today," Pete added. "Can he have the day off, too? We've only got one car."

The sergeant looked at them, then shrugged. Pete bought a flower arrangement with a stork and baby shoes on top, and he and Paul sped noisily out to the Island.

He selected St. Patrick's Day, a Sunday in the third month of Billy's life, for the baptism. To accommodate 200 guests, he reserved the banquet room of the Glass Bar, a Copiague catering spot. He planned a fast-paced evening of food, dancing and drinking, featuring a singer who specialized in bawdy songs.

Billy's birth had been a proud moment, but it also brought Pete the distractions babies are capable of. Like most new fathers, he had trouble giving up his former life: late movies, pizza at 2 A.M., impulsive outings. Yet this tiny, noisy presence altered everything. He hadn't expected such a change in Helen. She wouldn't go out, and she wouldn't bring in sitters. She didn't trust them. Pete tried to be understanding; inevitably, he became angry. One night he wanted to go to a nightclub in Manhattan. They hadn't gone out for weeks; Helen refused.

They fought bitterly. He consoled himself afterward that he still had Paul. And, of course, Marge. But it wasn't the same. Paul was not always available—he had family pressures, too. And nights out with Marge had to be hidden, or at least confined to places where he wouldn't be seen. An evening with Helen had no such pressures. He could drink and laugh with other cops and their wives legitimately. He felt he deserved this—it was bad enough to be condemned to sentry duty. Now he was stuck at home.

The singer had everyone in good humor by the end of the evening. Pete felt exceptional. He was stuffed with food and liquor, enjoying the toasts made by Paul and others. Now they caught him by surprise and formed a circle around his new family to sing an affectionately fractured version of *He's Got the Whole World in His Hands*. Pete felt a rush of tears. To hide them, he fled to the bar. Where he saw Victorio Sanchez!

The gunman stood before him in a tuxedo. Pete realized what he hadn't fully understood before, that Sanchez was *playing* with him. The black tuxedo's theatricality was unsurpassed. Sanchez said nothing. He had a date, a dark Puerto Rican girl who stood at the bar, hiding her face.

"You weren't invited!" Pete heard himself scream. "You shouldn't be here!" He bayed at his tormentor like a wounded bull. "You can't stay! I didn't invite you!"

He ran toward the banquet room to find Paul.

CHAPTER 12

SOMETHING was terribly wrong. Paul knew that much, but he felt helpless and confused He saw the fear in Pete's eyes, but it made no sense to him. He tried to move closer to Pete and found it impossible. The problem, whatever it was, didn't fit into any pattern Paul could undersand.

Even now, he hoped it was a joke. It *had* to be. Sanchez wouldn't show up at a private party. It was absurd. He checked with the district attorney's office yet another time. The gunman was still in jail.

Yet Pete insisted Sanchez was out. And his fear seemed genuine.

Or else this was the most elaborate, most tenacious, most dedicated super-goof ever attempted. Paul had to hold back. He couldn't fall for it.

Christ, he just didn't know! There was another possibility,

and he'd considered it, thinking of words like "paranoid," wondering if he should talk to Pete. But how do you talk to a friend about something like that? He couldn't. Pete was out there with those big frightened eyes, and Paul couldn't get there.

"Pete, come on," he said in exasperation at the christening. "What the hell would he be doing *here?*"

"He wants to kill me." The face was gray and frightened.

"Now wait a minute. Come on outside where we can talk." Paul looked carefully over his shoulder as they walked out. He saw nothing unusual in the bar—he didn't expect to.

"Pete." He caught himself. "Pete, what are you doing?"

He stopped again, trying to appear thoughtful, brotherly, even understanding. "Pete, there's nobody in the bar who looks like Sanchez, and no one is outside. This is no place to fool around. What's happening, anyway?"

But he saw his friend withdraw into a vast space behind mournful eyes.

"Paul, he was there. I don't make mistakes like this. I saw him. He must have run out the door when I went to find you." And Pete withdrew totally. He said nothing more. They returned to the party in uncomfortable silence.

Helen had become equally uncomfortable. Pete's depressions (caused, she'd thought initially, by his transfer) came startlingly often now and they lasted a long time. He was impossible during them. No conversation, no explanations: his gloom covering the house like a black flag.

Just before Billy was born, Helen had received a strange phone call.

"Is your husband home?" a voice asked. Callers usually asked for "Pete" or "Patrolman Bon Viso" and identified themselves. But when Helen asked who it was, she heard only breathing. Then a heavy click.

She assumed the call was a mistake. A second one came in, and she decided to tell Pete.

"I'm getting these strange phone calls," she said casually after dinner. "Someone asks for you without saying your name. Then they hang up."

Pete jumped from his chair, glaring angrily at her.

"Get out of the house!"

"Pete, what are you talking about? I just took a bath. I'm setting my hair."

"Get the rollers and get the hell out of the house! Go over to Buddy and Cathy's and tell 'em something. GET OUT!"

Helen walked across the street in considerable confusion, rollers and all. She watched television silently until the phone rang and Pete told her to come back. He was calm on the surface when she returned, but he wouldn't talk about what had happened, and the following day he changed their phone number.

She began to wonder about the medallion. The night of the christening, Pete had decided to wear it outside his tuxedo. She'd protested. The medallion looked cheap; it was nothing she wanted her husband to wear in front of 200 friends and relatives. She had no idea why he was so attached to it in the first place. Pete became angry; he sulked all the way into the city.

That night she noticed he was drinking far more than usual. And then he sent her home alone with the baby, saying he'd meet her at the house. She was embarrassed when he failed to arrive for nearly an hour, delaying a small post-christening party and forcing her to ask Buddy and Cathy for the spare key to let herself in. And when Pete finally arrived he sat in a chair, hands between his knees, staring at the floor. Afterward, he prowled the house into the early hours of the morning.

Social engagements became virtually impossible. Her husband, once so full of laughter, sat woodenly, wringing his hands, avoiding conversation, staring at the floor. He wasn't rude. He poured drinks, he shook hands. Sometimes he made small talk and smiled. But he always became depressed again, looking so sad each time she thought *she'd* cry. He hasn't looked like this since his father died, she thought.

He began to lose interest in how he looked. Or was he trying to *change* how he looked? She couldn't be sure. He began to wear the oddest combinations of dungarees, sweatshirts and old tennis shoes: around the house, out to the store, even into the city. She found this especially strange, for she knew Pete as a supreme peacock. When they were teen-agers, he had spent whole paychecks on $200 suits and sleek expensive shoes. As an adult he dressed just as flamboyantly in knit shirts, flashy suits, expensive shoes. He was similarly vain about his hair. He had it cut and styled often, and Helen helped him brush it out in the mornings before he went to work.

But now he bought a jar of pomade and combed his hair into a ducktail, a style he would have called "greaseball." When he finally tired of this foul hairdo, it took her an hour to wash the grease out of his hair (and out of the

pillowcases and off the backs of chairs). Now he let his
mustache grow long and wispy.

He talked of shaving off his eyebrows.

"Pete, what's going *on?* Why do you want to do this?"

"Helen," he said, smiling in a way that always confused
her, "I hafta get a new disguise." It was a joke, sort of.
That was the way he played it.

"Come *on.* You kidding me or something?"

They were driving to work in Paul's red Pontiac convertible. It was two weeks since the christening.

"No, he was in my back yard. I fired at him."

"What! You fired at someone in your backyard!"

Paul sat bolt upright in his seat, staring over his steering
wheel. "Did you see his face?"

"Oh yeah, I saw the bastard, no question."

"Are you *sure* who it was?"

"I'm sure, Paul. It was Sanchez. He came running across
the back yard, and I fired at him."

Paul's thoughts scattered like frightened deer. Jesus,
there's a schoolyard back there! Did Pete accidentally fire
at some passerby? This isn't good. This isn't good at all!
Holy shit! He watched Pete nervously from the corner of his
eye until they reached the city.

A week passed. Pete and Helen gave a small dinner
party.

"Hey, Helen . . ." Paul had followed her into the kitchen
so they could be alone. "Helen, what's this about someone
in your backyard?" Paul caught himself in embarrassment.
"Did Pete, uh . . . shoot at a burglar?"

Helen turned to him nervously.

"He didn't say it was a burglar." She stopped, mildly shocked at what she was going to say. She was about to talk about Pete *as if something was wrong with him.* He was taking weapons into the backyard nearly every day, refusing to tell her why. And he had a new word: "pressure." If she asked about the job, why he kept his guns so close, or what caused his moodiness, he answered, "pressure." He repeated it in bursts, throwing it out like a string of firecrackers.

"Pressure, pressure, pressure, *pressure.*"

Helen looked at Paul anxiously.

"He said someone was trying to kill him." She felt she was betraying Pete by saying even this.

"Do you remember the guy's name?" Paul was asking questions like a cop now.

"He said it, but I don't remember it." She moved some dishes around looking down at her hands. She'd heard the pistol shot, a tiny *pop,* from her kitchen. She'd called out to Pete as he stalked past her on his way upstairs. He'd shot at a squirrel, he said vaguely. Then he marched downstairs cradling his shotgun and ordered her to turn off the lights. For more than an hour she'd tried to help him by watching windows, quite ignorant of what she should be looking for. He said nothing about any "burglar" until the morning.

"Was it a Spanish name?" Paul asked.

At the precinct, Paul had watched Pete drop to one knee to reenact the scene. Pete described how the gunman had jumped from behind the woodpile, running at a wide angle to outflank him as if Pete were in some crazy Western movie and the outlaw was about to turn, draw, and fire. Except that Pete was the good guy. Pete had drawn his pistol and dropped to his knee and fired first; and the bullet had crunched harmlessly into a trash barrel. But it seemed to scare Sanchez enough to keep him running.

As Paul listened, watching his partner's face in the re-telling, he understood finally that . . . something was wrong. And he had decided to approach Helen.

"It *was* sort of a Spanish name," Helen said. "It sounded Italian, too."

Paul let it out slowly.

"Victorio Sanchez?"

"*Yes,* that's it."

In that moment, Helen wanted to kill Sanchez, whoever he was. *Anything* to bring Pete back.

Helen couldn't breathe. She gasped and struggled in her sleep, clawing her way out of dark dreams. She felt hands around her neck. She started to scream, and she awoke and realized she was in bed.

A man was trying to choke her. It was her husband.

"Tell me!" he screamed at her with closed eyes. "Tell me, you bastard!" And in that moment she could not move him. He held her like an executioner.

"Pete!" she screamed. "Pete! Pete!"

He stopped, suddenly awake. He watched her with dead eyes. His face was as gray and flat as stone.

Pete sat up in the bed and stared at Helen, then around him in the dark room. He could not believe his life had come to this. How could he face her in the morning? She lay next to him in the bed, crying softly, and he thought of how terrible his life had become. He *had* to find Sanchez. He had to end this—he couldn't bear it any longer.

"I'm sorry," he said haltingly. He held her, and she said something, and soon they were asleep.

CHAPTER 13

HE felt isolated. His friends, increasingly unnerved by his gloom, were becoming distant. His closest friends—Paul and Catherine, Buddy and Cathy —now came to his house only when asked. And he *hated* being alone. He needed the laughter and reassurance of social relationships; he needed people around him. He realized he was driving them away, and this upset him.

He focused his fear on Paul. Months earlier, he'd embarrassed his friend during a drinking bout by turning a complicated story about Helen into a pathetic confession of his own. Helen had complained that *she* cared more. *He* didn't take their love as seriously.

Paul looked at him blankly.

"I'm referring that to us," Pete said plaintively.

Paul shifted uncomfortably in his seat. "You know I'd do anything for you—just like you'd do anything for me."

"Yeah, but you have a brother, I don't. Maybe you don't feel the same way about me as I feel about you."

Pete's eyes grew large with anticipation and fear. "It's not true," Paul said quickly. "I love my brother and all that." He stopped for a moment. "But he's almost eleven years older than me." Paul started to blush. "I'm closer to you, that's all."

Pete had relaxed and they'd returned to their drinking.

But Paul hadn't gotten over his habit of canceling social engagements at the last minute. Once it had been an irritant; now it became a prelude to Pete's darkest depressions.

On April 10th, Paul managed a more than usually disruptive cancellation. The Bon Visos had invited the Rossis to dinner. It was Easter week, and Helen, glad for Paul's steadying company, had prepared a festive meal: chicken and rice, a big salad, a large pitcher of iced Sangria. Pete brought home a stuffed Easter bunny for one of Paul's children; he put out his best liquor.

And the phone rang.

Paul was apologizing. One of his children was sick—Catherine didn't want to leave the boy. They were due to arrive in an hour, and Pete began to burn. For a moment he blamed Catherine, since he was convinced that she worked constantly to come between them. Then his fury turned inward. He slammed down the phone.

They arrived at work a day later separately and silently. Pete brought in the dinner's flotsam: the stuffed bunny, a

houseplant Helen had planned to give to Catherine, clothing Paul had left at Pete's dry cleaners.

"Open your trunk," he said grimly, and like a grave-
digger he solemnly deposited the plant, the bunny, the
clothing. Paul motioned equally silently to Pete's trunk
and put in his gifts. They walked wordlessly inside the old
building where a cop at the front desk said they had a
walking post on the Bowery. Pete cursed loudly at the news;
it was a wet, foggy night. They went to their lockers in
the dark hallway, changed clothes and moved out.

The two friends stayed silent for an hour. They stalked
the decaying street in a self-imposed gloom, probing doorways with flashlights, watching winos and bums stumble
by on the littered avenue. Finally one man said something.
They traded a barrage of affectionate curses and the joy of
their friendship flamed up again. They laughed now and
talked with the winos and poor people they ran into, and
they bought drinks and toasted each other during their
meal break.

They were together again: but something remained off
center. Pete had one more drink, then another. He was
nervous; he'd been nervous all night, keeping the black
beaded medallion fully outside his summer blouse. A Fifth
Precinct sergeant had stopped them and ordered it off, but
Pete laughed and sidestepped the issue. He sat in the restaurant and tried to turn his thoughts elsewhere. It was no
use. Finally they headed back to the dark, half-empty headquarters building. It was midnight.

They passed a sleepy cop at the front desk and walked
down the half-lit hallway which twisted to the right.

Lamps of pre-war vintage hung down from a high ceiling on long black chains, casting a harsh light. Tall military-green lockers lined one side of the narrow passage. The passageway, in turn, led to back offices belonging to Nadjari's investigators, all empty now. About fifteen feet ahead there was a waist-high metal railing blocking the back area. The empty offices behind it were covered by partitions of frosted glass.

Pete started to undress. He and Paul were alone in the gloomy hall. He opened his locker, put his hat on the top shelf and pulled out a hanger. He buckled his gun belt into a circle and hung it from a hook. He lifted the medallion carefully over his head and looped it gently over yet another hook. He started unbuttoning his shirt.

"I'll be upstairs taking a shower," Paul said behind him.

They sometimes used a deserted shower room on the second floor which had belonged to a deputy commissioner. Paul padded out of the hallway in his slippers and underwear, leaving Pete alone.

Pete was in his underwear when he heard the first noise. The wind, he figured. He'd pulled on his civilian pants when he heard another sound. A rat? He glanced around his open locker door, which shielded him against the shadowy area down the hall and saw nothing. He bent down to pull on his shoes. He had no sense of danger.

Again. The noise.

Pete leaned around the locker door, suddenly suspicious. Shadowy light from the ancient lamps above him played off the distant metal and glass partitions. The space seemed to return his gaze. He turned back to his locker, smothering what he felt.

Something moved.

He whirled toward the alcove. He saw the pistol barrel immediately: a black snake emerging from behind the doorway, pushing slowly, almost hesitantly, aimed to the right of him.

Pete watched in silent fascination. He was astonished. Here! He'd have his showdown *here!* Like a mongoose, frozen, waiting, he watched the cobra unfold itself. The dark silhouette of the gun was visible now—the hand holding it seemed to be emerging from the earth, disembodied, bathed in shimmering black light.

The whole of Sanchez appeared before him in the passageway. The gunman's eyes were aflame, and the hallway seemed almost clouded as he stepped away from the wall casting that aura of strange light, swinging the pistol around like a blacksnake whip. He hadn't *pointed* it at Pete before. Pete's enemy stood behind the waist-high railing, black coat opened like a sail in the wind.

And then Pete came alive.

In a heartbeat, he pivoted toward the locker. He reached for his off-duty pistol and dropped to one knee, unsheathing the gun with a snap of its safety lock as he went down, reaching out with both arms, one hand closed around the small pistol, the other springing up to brace it.

And he began to fire.

He pulled at the pistol almost blindly, firing so fast that two shots burst before he reached the floor. By the time he was fully on his knees, his gun was empty.

The gunman simply lurched sideways and fell without firing: no screaming, nothing.

In that half-second's rage and confusion, Pete was engulfed by the sound of his bullets, the thunder of his pounding heart. He had faced the other man and triumphed! His first bullet missed. But he'd seen the second round crash into Sanchez's chest and knock him back. He'd watched the third and fourth plunge into Sanchez's hateful face, all crimson eruptions now. The man was down, a mass of spasms and blood on the floor. Half of him protruded from one end of the metal railing like a butchered pig.

Pete broke open the small Smith and Wesson and reloaded. The used shell casings cascaded to the floor.

He stepped away from the locker and walked toward his fallen enemy, who quivered and jerked before him. Pete stood calmly above him and braced himself, aiming for Sanchez's head. Pow! The bullet hit low, slamming into his enemy's shoulders. The dying man jerked convulsively. Pow-pow-pow-pow! Pete emptied his weapon as if he were firing a small Gatling gun.

He was flushed with rage, fear and triumph, and in that moment his life was defined. He was born anew as if a rogue thunderbolt had split him into Siamese twins.

Paul was standing behind him. For several seconds, the partner simply stared.

"What the fuck is the matter with you!" Paul screamed. "Are you *crazy* or something!"

Pete turned to his partner joyously.

"Paul! Paul! I killed him—I finally got the motherfucker! I shot Blackie!"

Paul was only shocked and confused.

And as Pete saw this, his own ecstasy turned to ice.

"Let's go," he bleated. "Let's get outta here." He was suddenly, deeply frightened. He did not look at Sanchez. He wanted only movement now, as if the walls of this back corridor might cave in like a mine tunnel. He threw on his clothes as Paul, still reeling from what he'd seen, instinctively stooped and gathered up the scattered shell casings.

Pete was half out of the winding coridor. Paul's head spun wildly as he dressed. This is trouble, he thought grimly, saying it again for emphasis. *This is trouble.* I'm in it. I'm here. The joke has gone too far . . .

The front desk guard, one of the Dozen, had obvious questions as they walked by.

"Charley, you didn't hear anything," Pete said conspiratorily. "Right?" And Charley Adams nodded, loyally joining up without knowing what conspiracy he'd joined.

In the car, Pete reloaded in silence, dropping shell casings on the floor, concentrating fiercely on the gun.

"Hey," Paul said tentatively. "You okay?" Pause. "Do you want me to go with you?"

Pete looked at him blankly. "No, no, I'm fine. I'm going to my mother's house." His face began to burn in the half-lit car, but he turned away. "Don't worry about me."

"I'll go with you if you want." Paul felt strange, disconnected things closing in. Pete seemed to be hiding from him. He asked again: "Do you want me to stay with you until you get to your mother's?"

"No, I feel safe now," Pete said in a calm, flat voice. "He's dead. Everything's all right."

Paul could not comprehend what he was hearing.

"I'll just go to my mother's," Pete said. "He won't be coming after me now."

Paul walked to his own car to return to Long Island. He couldn't think of anything else to do.

Pete sped downtown on a crest of turbulent emotions. He pushed in and out of traffic brashly, ignoring stop signs and red lights more bullishly than usual, enjoying new sensations: freedom, safety, his life renewed. Sanchez was dead!

The wave crashed. Jesus, I've killed him, he thought suddenly, grabbing at the wheel. Maybe I'm going to jail!

The fear reached out for him. He punched the car's throttle harder, almost in panic, taking a corner on squealing tires. Why didn't I get the gun? The street lamps and neon signs rushed at him. Why didn't I do things more carefully? Why didn't I get some evidence? This is crazy. I was actin' like a hit man or something.

And then, abruptly, he brought it down.

Shit, I didn't get it, that's all. He aimed the car like a bullet toward his mother's apartment. I didn't get the evidence I shoulda got. Nothing I can do—*nuthin'*.

He ran upstairs toward Rose's apartment as though someone were behind him. He turned the lock in a speedy metallic panic.

Rose Bon Viso looked up. Pete rarely came home this early.

"Whatsa matter?"

"Nothing."

"You're early."

Rose was accustomed to seeing Paul, too. "What's the matter? Where's Paul?"

"Paul has a different shift tomorrow. He went home." Pete avoided his mother's eyes.

"You want tea?" Rose watched her son like an old eagle. "How about eggs? You want steak? I got steak in the refrigerator."

Pete slumped into a kitchen chair, staring at his hands. "No, Ma, I'm not hungry." He asked for fruit juice and took an allergy tablet. He said nothing more.

"You wanta sandwich, maybe?" Rose assumed he'd had a fight with Paul. She knew nothing of Sanchez.

"Ma, I'm goin' to bed now."

He closed the bedroom door and walked to the window, staring out of it. The night was warm now. He undressed and pulled back the bedsheet—and shuddered. He began to shiver as he lay on the bed. He pulled the bedcovers over his head, and hid in their heat. Rolled up like a ball, he fell asleep.

Paul had reached the second-floor landing by the time he heard the first volley. He was padding downstairs in his slippers, shirtless, carrying his towel and soap dish.

Firecrackers?

He had counted five rounds and knew that he'd heard bullets. An ambush? The Black Liberation Army? He froze. Then he heard another splatter of gunfire. And silence.

He waited a few seconds more and heard no reaction to the noise, neither shouting nor commotion. He tiptoed downstairs and turned toward the back hallway.

He found his best friend standing proudly in the corridor with a smoking gun.

"My mind was spinning a million miles an hour," he remembered later. "I didn't put any of it together. I knew there would be trouble, and I had to help Pete."

He gave no thought to reporting the incident. He simply scooped up the shell casings, dressed and left.

Friday morning. Pete lay under the covers and wrestled with his fear. His anxiety felt like the blankets: tousled, undefined, binding. Sanchez, of course, was dead—but it might cost him his job. He'd be penalized for killing someone "without justification"—killing a man and not doing "the right thing" afterward. He rolled hurriedly out of bed to call the Fifth Precinct.

"This is Bon Viso," he said in a low, cautious voice. "I hafta go to court. I'm going straight there." The precinct didn't object. No problems yet . . .

In the kitchen, he turned down Rose's offer of eggs, taking coffee and an English muffin as she watched him in silence. He drove hurriedly to the courthouse, switching off his mind as much as possible.

He stopped at Cal's. It was shortly after 9 A.M. and he planned to go to court next. But he got back in the car. He shouldn't go to court, he decided. He remembered a cousin who worked in Central Park. He decided to go to the park.

He sped uptown and parked in a garage on 59th Street. He walked to Wollman Skating Rink where the cousin worked. His relative was in another part of the park, and a workman directed him there. It was a bright, warm day. Pete began walking.

The late hour—it was 6 o'clock now—caught him by surprise. He'd walked a great distance, floating through the day on a cloud—it was all he remembered. His clothes were soiled, and he felt clammy from sweat and dust, as if he might have been sitting or lying down. He walked to a phone booth on 59th Street and called Helen.

"Where are you?" she asked him immediately.

He didn't want to say.

"Is there something wrong?"

He mumbled something.

"Paul called. He said if you come home, we shouldn't stay. He said get in the car and come straight to his house."

Pete answered slowly. "Did he . . . say why?"

"Something about Internal Affairs."

"Where's Paul now?" Pete talked slowly and evenly.

"He says IAD has him."

Nonchalantly: "Okay. Thank you."

"Pete?"

"Yes?"

"Has something happened?"

"I don't wanna talk about it now." He was briefly silent. "You'll be all right there. I'll call you later." Pete drew in his breath sharply. "I'm not coming home just yet."

And he hung up.

He called the old headquarters building to find Paul. Paul was at Internal Affairs.

"What post was he supposed to have?" Pete worked to get his thoughts together.

"I don't know," a voice said. "He came in to change, and they scooped him up."

When he put down the phone, Pete knew he smelled bad. He realized that his clothes were soaked with sweat. The secret apartment was nearby, and he turned toward it. As day became dusk, he still walked in a dream.

He called Helen from the apartment—her greeting seemed oddly muffled.

"Anybody there?" he asked quickly.

"Yes . . ."

"Who?"

Silence.

"New York Ciy?"

"Yes."

"Bosses?"

"Hold on." She turned away. "Lieutenant, what was your name again?"

"More than one?" he asked.

"Two of them."

Jesus! Two lieutenants from IAD!

"All right, sweetheart," he said shakily. "I'm not coming home now." Pause. "Get 'em out of there, okay? They've got no business being in the house. Tell 'em you've got something to do."

"They just walked in." She tried to reassure him. "They weren't staying."

"Are they being gentlemen?" He had to know. The IAD sometimes acted like gangbusters. They treated cops *worse than criminals.* "Sweetie, get their names and take the message," he said, ringing off.

He called again. They were parked outside now, Helen said. He was to call headquarters "forthwith."

"Sweetheart," he said like a character in an old spy movie. "I was gonna come home, but I don't wanna come home just now. I'll keep in telephone communication."

He went on. "If they leave, walk out and make sure they've left the entire block."

"All right, Pete."

"Everything okay with you? How's the baby?"

"Everything's fine." Another pause. "Are you all right?"

"Oh yeah, I'm fine. Don't worry."

"Take care of yourself."

"Okay, thank you."

He called old headquarters again: Paul hadn't returned. Fear, now anger, filled him. Men waited for him, and he was alone, and they wanted to take him somewhere. If they did it wrong, he'd have to fight them.

He *hated* those IAD people. The phone rang.

"Kid, how are you?"

"Oh Paul!" A lifeline. "I'm glad it's you—what's happening?"

"I can't talk now."

"I heard you were at IAD."

"Yeah, I'm still there."

"What happened?" Pete began to feel the tension.

"They wanna know some things." Pause. "What are *you* doing?"

"Well, I'm up here, you know? I don't know what to do—they're out at my house."

"Then don't go. If you want, I'll send Catherine to pick up Helen. You can go straight to my house."

"I . . . don't know." Pete did not feel he could move, yet. "Lemme see what happens."

"Okay, but don't let 'em snatch you up."

"I'll be here a little while longer, Paul." Pete desperately didn't want to let go. "If you want to get in touch with me . . ."

"Yeah, but I don't know if I'll be able to." Paul's voice faded suddenly. "I've got to get off now."

"All right, Paul. So long."

He was deeply frightened. They had Paul, and they were closing in. He called Helen.

"They gone?"

"Yes . . ."

". . . Good."

"Not so good. Two Suffolk County detectives were here. They acted like they owned the house. One was on the couch, reading the newspaper, making himself comfortable."

Pete listened in horrified fascination.

"They said they were waiting for you. I said, 'You're not waiting in this house. I've got things to do—get out!' One said: 'But your husband's a policeman. We're policemen.' 'Get out of my house,' I said, 'you understand? I don't want you here!' "

"They still on the block?"

"Yeah, they're outside in a car."

"Everything else all right?"

"Yes."

"Listen, I'm not coming home yet . . ."

"Don't worry, just do what you have to do." Helen

seemed very bold now. "And don't do anything silly. Call me when you can."

He called her every hour. At midnight, the Suffolk car was gone.

"They wanted to know what kind of car you have."

"What'd you say?"

"I said you had a blue Rambler."

"Very good. You did the right thing." For a moment he felt relief. "I'm coming home now. I should be there in an hour."

The drive to Long Island spooked Pete badly. He drove the dark gold Maverick cautiously. By the time he reached Suffolk County, he realized he was behaving like a criminal. When radio cars passed by, he crouched low behind his steering wheel, deeply frightened.

It seemed almost funny. As a cop, he was usually indifferent to society's marginal laws. He avoided traffic tickets simply by showing his shield. That special paranoia of the average citizen—fear that the law will reach out for you unexpectedly—was nothing to him. Cops were his family.

Until tonight.

I'm the hunted, he thought melodramatically, not the hunter.

He pulled up short of his block, got out and walked to its corner. In the darkness, he scanned the long block. Seeing nothing, he drove halfway down and pretended to walk to the home he'd parked in front of. No one approached him. Carefully, he turned and walked toward his own house.

It was Saturday morning, about 2 A.M., and Helen saw

Pete standing before her, shaking with fear. His skin glistened with perspiration—"eyes almost out of his head," she remembered later.

The tears came in a rush. "Hold me," he cried. "Please, hold me."

And they fell to the couch, where he shook and sobbed in her arms. "I've got something to tell you," he choked. And he talked of Sanchez and the dark gun. And what had happened—bullets flying in the ancient corridor, Paul's panic, *his* panic as they left the building, the feelings of loss and isolation that next morning, his escape to Central Park.

Helen began to cry, too. "Take it easy—take it easy," she pleaded. "Everything will be all right." Sanchez *was* dead, Pete insisted. He had nothing to worry about there. But his job—he might lose it. And perhaps he'd go to jail. They were coming; he couldn't run. Besides, his pay would stop, and Helen and the baby would be left to fend for themselves.

He was trapped.

He fled into the bathroom. Helen waited, composing herself.

She became aware of the bathroom's silence.

She found Pete sitting in the tub, fully clothed. He was behind the shower curtain, staring at his hands, staring past them at something she could not see.

"Come outta there," she said. "Come outta there and talk to me."

"Leave me alone . . ."

Five minutes passed slowly, and Pete emerged; and they talked. Pete agreed to call the department now, as instructed. A sharp voice on the telephone said to report to IAD headquarters in Brooklyn at 8 A.M. "sharp." Pete instinctively asked for the man's name and shield number. Then he ate some cold chicken and drank a Fresca and went to bed.

CHAPTER 14

PAUL's day had been equally difficult. Driving to work, he thought constantly about the previous night. When he arrived at the old headquarters, he saw a photo and fingerprinting laboratory parked outside. He parked and walked into the building and saw detectives and ballistics men everywhere. Casually, he asked one of the Dozen what had happened.

"Some crazy bastard shot up the building last night."

Paul professed moderate disinterest and walked slowly to his locker in the back hallway. He saw people pulling bullets from the far wall, dusting for fingerprints, marking other walls with chalk. Twenty minutes later, he was walking the same Bowery post he and Pete had had the previous night. But this time his partner, a heavy-set Irishman named Mike, seemed kind of . . . tense. Paul grew nervous.

He spotted an unmarked patrol car. They were getting ready for the snatch, he figured. Defiantly, he walked into a barbershop. He was laid out in the chair when he saw the car outside. Paul smiled, enjoying his moment of rebellion. I might as well look good, he figured.

A squad car pulled up. "Get in, Rossi," said a sergeant.

"What's happening, Sarge?"

"We're taking you to Internal Affairs."

"Is this about last night's incident?"

The sergeant nodded. In the car, Paul lapsed into silence, and soon they reached the Brooklyn Bridge.

He would tell them the truth, he was thinking. He would tell them Pete had a "problem"—that he'd tried to help, that it had been going on quite a while, that . . .

They wouldn't believe it. Besides, he had to protect Pete.

The car was in Brooklyn now, and he knew what he had to do.

He'd deny everything. He'd make the head-hunters work for their information. He didn't like them any better than Pete did. They'd forgotten what it was like to be on the street—what it was like to *care* about your partner. He resolved to make them sweat, and while the car rolled on, he thought briefly about what they might do to him in return. It would be bad.

It was after five o'clock when the patrol car arrived at IAD headquarters; by now, Pete was nearing the end of his mindless odyssey in Central Park. The building resembled the dungeon Paul had imagined, a decaying old fortress with steel gates and special doors. Gates locked loudly behind him. The elevator took him to the third floor, where he was ushered into a shabby waiting room. A lieutenant appeared and ceremoniously took his gun, a perfect moment of psychological warfare.

Paul stared at his empty holster, watching it swing free. He was badly unnerved. Then he caught himself.

IAD cops walked by his little room, and they looked in and talked among themselves. "That's Rossi?" he heard them ask. And they nodded and smiled—or scowled—among themselves. Paul sat in the waiting room with his empty holster, hating them. They were playing! Half an hour passed. A voice: "Joe, you ready to talk to him yet?" Another voice: "Yeah." Two cops came to the room. "All right, officer, come with us." Paul rose, bloated with fear and anticipation. A voice: "We're not ready yet." And Paul sat down, his heart racing.

It happened four times.

After a third time, he turned on the room's television set, loud. *Ben Hur* was playing, and he gave it rapt attention. But his inquisitors had done their work: Paul's mind spun wildly out of control.

An hour later, they came for him. The chief wanted to speak to him. Curiosity roused Paul. He'd never been this close to a chief inspector.

The chief, a small red-faced balding man with bulging eyes, sat behind a table in a small conference room. Behind him, Paul counted two captains, two lieutenants, two sergeants and one patrolman (probably for muscle, he figured).

The chief looked at him out of puffy eyes. He said the

conversation was unofficial, nothing would be on tape. He'd been in touch with Mr. Nadjari's office, he added. The prosecutor seemed willing to let the department handle this. Nadjari wouldn't prefer criminal charges if the department resolved things.

Nadjari? Paul was confused. Why would the special prosecutor care? This was no corruption case. It was an "unauthorized expenditure of ordinance"—Pete shot up a hallway, that's all.

I can't make promises, the chief was saying, standing up. But if the officers involved in last night's incident were to *volunteer* the correct information, they'd probably receive nothing more than a 30-day "rip." That would mean no pay for 30 days, maybe a year's probation. The chief walked around the table now. He couldn't promise it, Paul was to understand, but it probably would happen . . . if the officers who were involved came forward.

The chief was about three inches in front of Paul now, staring up at him. It seemed a very, very long speech. "All I want to know," the chief was saying . . .

Paul braced himself.

". . . is if you or anyone you know had anything to do with the shots fired in police headquarters last night."

"Chief," Paul said finally in a low voice. "I want a lawyer."

Paul thought the man would turn purple. He saw blood vessels swelling in the chief's neck. He heard a collective sigh from the other men in the room. They would get tough now. But he'd set his course, and he resolved to stick to it. *He would not betray Pete.* It was all he knew.

They sent him back to *Ben Hur.*

A cop asked for his locker combination. They wanted his off-duty gun. For ballistics, the cop said. He was told that a Patrolmen's Benevolent Association lawyer would be coming.

But when the lawyer arrived, Paul disliked him immediately. He was a tall, nervous Irishman, and Paul figured that Italians and Jews were the best lawyers. Besides, the guy was an ex-cop, a middle-aged man with an acne-scarred face. He looked dumb—and whose side was he on?

"I don't know anything," Paul insisted when the Irishman started asking questions. The lawyer went off to talk to the chief inspector. Paul asked a captain in the outside corridor if he could make a phone call.

"Who you calling?"

"Dial-a-joke." Pause. Boyish smile. "I need something to cheer me up."

The captain grimaced at him.

"Dial-a-prayer?" Paul smiled. He called Helen and hurridly instructed her to take the baby and go to his house when Pete arrived. "Trust me," he said, ringing off.

He was taken to another conference room containing the same cast of inquisitors, minus the chief inspector. A tape recorder hummed alongside, and Paul stood before them stiffly.

"State your name, rank, shield number and command," someone said.

"Paul Rossi, shield number 28776, Ninth Precinct on temporary assignment to the Fifth Precinct," he began mechanically. He insisted he'd seen nothing. He was told of General Order 15. His interrogation was a departmental matter, not a criminal proceeding. He could not refuse to answer questions, or he'd be suspended.

They asked why he went upstairs to take a shower. "I was dirty," he said tersely.

"What was Bon Viso doing?"

"He was getting dressed."

"Who left the building first?"

"Pete did."

"Did Police Officer Adams saying anything to you?"

"No."

"Did you see any shooting?"

"No."

"Did you hear any shooting?"

"No."

By the end of it, Paul had repeated the word "no" at least fifteen times. The cop who'd been at the old headquarters front desk, Charley Adams, was brought in to identify Paul. The questions from stern faces around the semi-circle continued. And finally, it was over, and he was taken back to the waiting room where *Ben Hur* was no longer playing. He went to the telephone and called the secret apartment on a hunch, finding Pete.

Eventually he was taken to the Fifth Precinct, where he waited until the ballistics unit had finished with his guns. Paul arrived at the old headquarters close to midnight and maintained a brittle silence as members of the Dozen crowded around.

"What the hell did you guys *do*?"

"Nothing. Nothing at all."

"Cut the bullshit. We saw the IAD."

"I told you. We didn't do anything. Nothing happened, you understand?"

But he was aware that his life had changed. He and Pete would not be partners again; he knew it. Avenue C, the good times, the pranks, nights in the bars, the streetcorner detective work—all of it was gone. For the first time, he felt the growing weight of his life.

A lieutenant from Internal Affairs stood by the door. The lieutenant was lean and gray-haired, wrapped in a dark trenchcoat, and Paul noticed that the man's left eye was badly bloodshot, so much so that Paul in future moments of defiance would describe him as "the lieutenant with the red eye" at departmental inquiries. He stood in Paul's path.

"You were involved, Rossi," the lieutenant growled at him. "What you told them in Brooklyn is gonna screw you up more."

"You don't know what you're talking about," Paul retorted, trying to avoid the cop's eyes.

"It was either you or your buddy. We know that."

"Who are you talking about?"

"Bon Viso."

"You're right. He *is* my buddy."

"You think you're cute, right?" The lieutenant's bad eyes seemed to flash at Paul like a traffic light. "Being cute don't pay, you know?"

Paul felt himself stiffen. "Everybody's gotta do what they gotta do," he said curtly. And he walked into the night. It was Friday at midnight, 24 hours before Easter Sunday.

The New York Post's weekend edition hit the streets

early that Saturday with a banner headline that answered Paul's questions about the special state prosecutor:

GUARD NADJARI AFTER THREATS

Below the headline, a front-page story told of extra bodyguards being assigned to the prosecutor "following several telephone threats that someone was going to shoot him." Nadjari had received four threats in three weeks, the paper continued. Two agents guarded him full time now.

"*The Post* learned of the special guard," the story continued, "following the mysterious middle-of-the-night spate of gunfire inside the former Police Headquarters at 240 Centre Street yesterday. Nine shots were fired . . . six slugs ripped through (the) 20-foot glass and steel partition wall" of an office "used secretly for the past five weeks by a special unit from Nadjari's office."

That Saturday morning, Pete and Paul hadn't read *The Post,* and they suspected nothing of their considerable fame.

"The special squad," the story went on, "was using that office to question possible figures in the theft of 398 pounds of narcotics from the police property clerk's office, which included the evidence found from the famous 1962 French Connection case." Both cops and mobsters had already been interrogated, it was explained, and while the investigations were secretive, "it was believed that most of the skeleton crew assigned to the former headquarters knew exactly why the special unit was there."

Not exactly. Patrolmen Rossi and Bon Viso didn't know, as they would later testify. The fact that his bullets (actually ten of them) had found the partitioned walls of Maurice

Nadjari's secret sub-offices meant nothing to Pete as he drove that morning to IAD headquarters.

"At first," the article added," it was believed that yesterday's shooting might have been a sort of warning to the special unit."

One reason the department believed this, of course, was that the mysterious gunmen had covered their tracks rather well. A sergeant and four detectives assigned to an organized crime unit working on the third floor of the old building had rushed downstairs after hearing the commotion.

"Just a couple of guys goofing around," Charley Adams had told them, elaborating on Pete's instructions slightly.

A civilian working in the basement photo lab had been badly frightened and had tried to reach Adams' security desk on the phone. Finally, according to *The Post,* he had called a detective he knew in Brooklyn. The detective called a precinct house near the old headquarters, which sent over a radio car.

"Everything's fine," Adams said.

The radio car called a supervising sergeant. Just a couple of cops goofing around, Adams said. And the car left.

The photo lab employee called his detective friend in Brooklyn again. The detective again called the local precinct, which again called Charley Adams and asked him to go downstairs and reassure the frightened lab technician. Which Charley did.

But Friday morning as Pete was beginning his dreamless trek through Central Park, an IAD detective assigned to the Nadjari unit came on duty and found his office riddled with bullets.

Saturday. Pete rose at 8 A.M. He was due at IAD headquarters at precisely that hour.

"No sense rushing it," he muttered grimly as he put on
a bulky red sweater, patched jeans, white socks and blue
tennis shoes. One of the dungaree patches announced: "Sex
—breakfast of champions." Another was crimson and heart-
shaped. He wore the beaded medallion, too.

Weeks earlier, Helen's mother had invited them to Easter
dinner. IAD headquarters was five blocks away from her
apartment, making it possible to combine a family holiday
and a professional catastrophe into one excursion. Pete
loaded the car with gifts, blankets and baby bottles, and
after gathering up Helen, the baby and the dog, he started
up the street.

Something in Pete still reaches for this moment. "We
were all together again," he explained years later without
elaborating. "The family was together."

Driving in, he turned on the radio and heard about the
"mysterious spate of gunfire." He tingled a bit at his fame.
He had his guns with him now. He had 1800 rounds of
ammunition and three pistols, and he knew the department
would ask for them. He gave Helen one of the guns, a tiny
.25 caliber automatic worn in an ankle holster, hoping to
hide it from the department.

On the third floor of the old headquarters he was met by
a captain who asked immediately for the guns.

Pete surrendered them slowly: first the off-duty revolver. He broke open its cylinder, dumped the bullets into
his hand, and probed the open chamber with his finger.
The captain reached for the gun and examined the weapon

as if he were near-sighted, sniffing it. Pete pulled a .22 pistol from the left side of his waistband, removed the clip and checked the barrel. The captain sniffed at this gun, too—like a dog, Pete thought.

They'd already taken his service revolver from the locker. The captain asked for the other gun listed on Pete's records, the .25 automatic.

"It's in my safe deposit box," Pete lied. "I use it in the summertime."

The captain showed Pete to the waiting room.

The tall Irish lawyer approached. He seemed friendly.

"Listen, Pete," he began almost conspiratorily. "I dunno what I'm gonna do with your partner. He was here yesterday, and he wouldn't talk." Pause. The lawyer had moved very close to Pete. "What *did* happen?"

"Well," Pete said, looking up, "I did it."

The lawyer was caught off guard. He looked at Pete. ". . . Uh, whatta you mean? You did, uh . . . what?"

A confession was apparently the last thing the lawyer expected. His head bobbed furiously. "You sure you weren't, uh . . . drunk? Maybe we can get to the department chaplain on this."

"No, no, I did it," Pete insisted now, enjoying his drama. "Lemme tell you about it." They sat down and Pete told him the story of Victorio Sanchez.

The lawyer listened nervously and paced about the small room.

Then he smiled broadly.

"That's great! You're crazy—that's great!" He almost laughed.

But Pete's face turned savagely dark, and he started to

advance menacingly. "Don't you *ever* call me crazy," he said angrily.

The lawyer stepped back. He seemed to Pete to be moving all parts of his body at once. "Easy, easy. Sit down, sit down. I'll be right back, I'll be right back. I gotta talk to someone."

The lawyer returned quickly. "Okay, okay, it's good. We're gonna talk in front of the tape now. There'll be some people there, but don't worry. I'll be right there. I'll object if there's something you shouldn't answer. Don't worry about a thing, kid. We're in good shape."

Pete began to sweat as if he were under a sun lamp. The room seemed very hot. His sweater seemed absurdly heavy, like a blanket. The lawyer reached out and put his arm around Pete's shoulders.

They walked down a long corridor crossed with offices. Pete watched the IAD men inside as he passed, hating them. He entered the conference room, where he counted a dozen men in a semicircle. Someone turned on a tape recorder, and Pete was told to identify himself: "Police Officer Peter J. Bon Viso, shield number 14205, Ninth Precinct, temporarily assigned Fifth Precinct."

"Tell us what happened," one of the commanders said.

"I did it."

"WHAT . . . ?"

It was as if he'd thrown a custard pie at them. The room exploded with coughing, double-talk, whispering and expressions of shocked indignation.

A voice said: "Officer, would you care to explain that?"

And Pete told them about Sanchez. He had three bullets in his pocket, and as he talked he reached in the pocket and fingered them like prayer beads. At first the room was absolutely still. Then they began to interrupt him. They asked questions and sent runners to check on what he was saying, sometimes before he finished saying it. Pete watched the IAD men scurry in and out, and he heard phones being dialed, other phones ringing, frantic conversations. When the tiny, bug-eyed chief snapped his fingers, someone rose to his feet and ran out. Pete was almost proud. He *loved* causing all this commotion.

And then it was over. He was red-faced and near tears by this time. The anguish and tension of a year's terror, a year of keeping it *in,* was finished. The tape recorder was shut down and he was sent back to the waiting room.

He waited fifteen minutes, utterly wrung out.

The lawyer walked in with a hangdog expression. "They don't believe you," he said. "They're gonna suspend you."

Pete felt oddly at peace with the decision. Eventually, he would grow bitter about it—but at that moment he honestly wondered if he would have believed such a story. Besides, you can't go around shooting people, even in self-defense.

The captain who'd taken his guns walked into the room. He stood before Pete and stated the time (13:15 hours), and the date (April 13, 1974), and finally the purpose of his visit: "Suspended, Internal Affairs Office—let me have your shield and I.D. card, officer."

Pete thought he might vomit. He struggled mightily to control himself, fumbling in his pocket for the leather strap his shield was pinned to. He pulled the green card from his wallet as if it were one of his organs. The shield and card had been in his pocket for five years. He gave them up and turned away from both men, hiding what he felt. Then he walked out of the room.

In the elevator, the lawyer said they wanted the .25 automatic. They didn't believe it was in a safety deposit box. IAD cops were coming to his mother-in-law's apartment. In despair, he asked that only one man accompany him inside ("I don't wanta make a scene in front of my mother-in-law, okay?") and they agreed. Grimly, he introduced the cop as "my friend, Harry" and turned away from Mary Woodrow as he gave "Harry" the tiny pistol. The door closed and he sat down. He watched the television set briefly. He got up.

"Listen," he said to both women. "I hafta get out of here." He called Paul, who was scheduled for a 4 P.M. tour, to arrange a rendezvous at the secret apartment.

He had no badge or gun now. As he drove, he began to think of bills: doctor bills, the mortgage, grocery bills. He was not off the force yet, but the suspension meant he was technically unemployed: no pay, no benefits. He was required to report in each week; and it would be impossible to find work with such an ambigious employment status. How would he pay his bills? *He had no paycheck now.*

A squad car appeared. He realized he'd run a red light on Fulton Street. It had happened countless times before. He reached for his shield to identify himself as a member of the brotherhood.

He suddenly realized he had nothing to show. The cop asked for his license and registration.

"Uh, officer, you have to forgive me," he began haltingly. "Please, I just got suspended." He showed him the leather casing, which now held only his service medals. "Uh, I was involved with that incident at 240 Centre Street. I'm sorry."

The cop let him go, patting him on the back, wishing him well. Pete pulled away from the curb, filled with marbled layers of rage and sadness.

He made it into Manhattan without further incident, picking up Marge Riley on the way so she might join the wake. Minutes after Pete arrived at the apartment, the phone rang.

"We're in the same boat," Paul told him.

He was suddenly very upset. *Paul hadn't killed anyone!* He wasn't involved! Pete nursed a drink and told the difficult story to Marge, who listened quietly, wondering what it really meant.

Paul arrived with the Dozen's supervising sergeant in tow. The sergeant seemed sympathetic, but after beer and sandwiches arrived and everyone settled down, he looked at them in a boozy, fatherly way.

"Hey, you guys," he said, "what really happened?"

Until he left, Pete and Paul assumed they were talking to a microphone.

Easter Sunday dawned wet and gray. The other relatives arrived; they'd heard. The Bon Visos and the Woodrows sat in the living room, playing small-change poker, drinking wine and talking as little as possible. Pete sat among them as if he were terminally ill. The family left him alone. The phone rang.

"How ya doin' kid?" Paul asked cheerfully. Something very interesting would be on the six-o'clock news. Paul had called a local television station, and the station had sent a camera crew out to his house.

For the first time that day, Pete became animated. He laughed happily when the television screen showed Paul perched nervously on his couch. Paul looked great! Pete watched his best friend tell the television newsman that his partner needed "help"; that Internal Affairs had been unfair, that the department had "turned its back," that . . .

Something frightening nudged at Pete.

Why hadn't Paul mentioned Sanchez? He remembered that the Internal Affairs people had asked him about Sanchez. *Where was the body?* They'd found nothing, no corpse, no gun. They asked why Pete hadn't confiscated the pistol. Was it possible that Sanchez was still alive?

No. He'd seen the gunman fall. He'd watched Sanchez absorb nine bullets. No human being could survive that. There had to be another explanation.

He winced when Paul said that Patrolman Bon Viso needed "help." What did he mean? Psychiatric help? It was embarrassing; his entire family was watching. Was his partner suggesting—on television, no less—that he might have—imagined the whole thing?

He'd been on the "psycho" the 10-54 runs often enough. He'd been in the ambulances. He'd gone into Bellevue Hospital with men and women who had to be restrained in handcuffs and strait jackets. *He was not like that!* He remembered the old man on the Bowery who ran back and forth frantically urinating on anyone he could reach. He remembered people laughing. He remembered how he caught himself when he was tempted to laugh—people had laughed at his crippled mother. He remembered as a boy holding her hand defiantly on shopping trips as she endured the heartless stares of ignorant people. How *humiliating* to suffer that, how terrifying to be a target of whispering . . .

For the first time in his life, he considered the possibility that he was insane.

CHAPTER 15

PETE reached for the telephone smelling of the shotgun's discharge. As he touched it, he saw his own trembling hands. Three times! At close range he'd fired his shotgun at the bastard *three times.* He dialed the local police slowly, choking back the froth of his emotions. He had to be calm. He reported—an armed prowler in his back yard. He'd fired at him. They should know that.

It was three days after his suspension.

A tall Suffolk cop with dark eyes and closely-cropped hair arrived now. He seemed sympathetic and Pete talked guardedly of himself and Sanchez. He was a New York City policeman, he explained—lately suspended. A man was trying to kill him. It was related to the department trouble. The man had been in his back yard minutes earlier, trying again. It was the gunman's second visit to Copiague.

Another knock on the door. A smaller cop, wiry and blond, came in. He brushed past Pete, scowling, and led Helen to the far side of Pete's living room. The larger cop remained polite, nodding, asking more questions; the smaller one interrogated Helen rapid-fire. Almost on cue, both cops asked to see the flood-lit back yard. Pete walked them out to the patio, stopping where he remembered firing first.

"What the fuck are you trying to pull?" the smaller cop demanded suddenly. He'd seen a shell casing in the grass about twenty yards away. "You shot from the patio? The shell's over *here?*"

Pete felt his head get hot. He turned angrily toward the smaller cop; then he became frightened. "I must have been mistaken," he said in a low, hateful voice.

"I've heard about you," the cop continued. "Don't pull this bullshit when I'm working."

Pete froze in place, and the other cop, sensing trouble, said something to his partner. The smaller one walked away.

They returned to the house, where Pete opened his briefcase to show them Sanchez's yellow sheet. It went back to 1962: burglary, assault, drugs, criminal mischief, more drugs. The big cop seemed to read it carefully.

"Did you see a car?"

Pete began to feel better. "No," he said, relaxing a little.

The big cop walked out to his car to broadcast a description of Sanchez. As he did, Helen reached for the phone to call Paul so he could explain what was really happening.

The blond cop stopped her.

"We've put a description of this guy on the air," he said

testily. "So just lock your doors. Call us if you see or hear anything."

He turned to Pete.

"And look, don't go outside again with your gun. Stay inside with your wife and child and protect them. Just *call us* if you hear anything."

And they left. Pete walked from window to window now, clutching his gun. Helen trailed behind him. She finally went upstairs, suggesting to no avail that he come too. He walked from window to window and watched with considerable satisfaction as Suffolk radio cars drove past the house at 45-minute intervals—he timed them—casting a spotlight on school yards, the trees, his yard. He stole about his house like a thief, wide-eyed in the darkness, checking doors, waiting for the Suffolk cars.

And finally, as dawn sweetened the darkness, he went upstairs and fell into an exhausted, uneasy sleep with the shotgun propped alongside the bed.

They had begun a series of meetings with the lawyer to prepare their case for reinstatement. Paul drove his car to Pete's house so they could ride in together. On the second morning, Pete became extremely upset.

"I don't like walking around with no gun," he said angrily. "I'm bringing one of mine."

Paul and Helen argued against this, and Pete seemed to give in. Both men climbed into Pete's car, and Pete wordlessly drove toward a nearby shopping center.

"Whatta you doing?"

"I wanta go a different way today." And saying this, Pete

abruptly stopped in front of a hardware store and jumped out of the car. Paul ran inside and found his friend buying a bolt-action 16 gauge shotgun and two hundred rounds of ammunition.

"Uh, Pete, don't you think that's a bit much? Two hundred rounds?"

Pete's eyes were dark with fear. "No, I need the ammunition in case I'm holed up someplace and I'm shooting it out with him."

"I thought Sanchez wasn't around anymore," Paul said tentatively.

"He's chased me before. If I see him this time, I'm gonna blow his fucking head off." Pete seemed almost to crackle as he talked. "I'm sick and tired of this shit! This guy can't keep chasing me!"

"Look, I'm with you, so don't worry."

With the shotgun in the trunk, they sped silently into the city. Paul's mind ran very fast.

"Let's have a drink at Cal's first," he said. 'I'll call the lawyer from there and make sure he's ready."

In the bar he went to the phone. With some difficulty, he explained to the lawyer that Pete was badly upset. Pete had a shotgun—there might be trouble. What could he do?

"Whatever you do," the lawyer answered, "don't bring him into *my* office with a shotgun."

For a brief moment, Paul thought the entire world was truly insane.

"Can't you give me a suggestion?" he asked weakly. "I don't want Pete to be in more trouble with the department. Should I call a hospital?"

"Stay there," the lawyer answered. "I'll call you back."
Twenty minutes passed. Desperately, Paul called the
lawyer again.

"Help is coming," the lawyer said. "I've talked to someone at the department."

The sergeant from the Dozen detail walked into the bar.
Paul thought nothing of it, since the sergeant was a regular
patron. Then a Fifth Precinct captain walked in. Suddenly
Paul knew that help had arrived; he raised his glass in a
silent toast to whatever was coming.

He moved over to brief the captain, then returned to
Pete and asked for his friend's car keys, saying that the
car was parked by a fire hydrant and might be towed. As
calmly as possible, Paul walked outside, pocketing the
trunk key so that the shotgun was out of reach.

The captain approached Pete and asked him to come to
the Fifth Precinct. Pete didn't understand this, but he agreed
to do it.

He found the lawyer there. It was very confusing. Suddenly they were asking if he had weapons or "contraband"
on him. He said he didn't; they began searching him, patting him down. They took a lock-blade street knife he routinely carried; then his shotgun clip. They *knew* about the
shotgun.

"Hey, Pete, whatta you say we take you to the hospital,"
the captain said. "We'd like you to talk to one of the doctors."

The confusion was getting worse.

"Whatta you talking about!" he said quickly. "I'm not
going anywhere—just leave me alone. I'm all right!"

The lawyer turned to him. "Pete, I think this might be a

good idea. Maybe you should go up there, okay?" Pete saw
that everyone was conferring.

"Let's go out for an ice cream or something," Paul said.
They found a Good Humor man and Paul bought him a
strawberry shortcake bar. Pete realized he was very hungry.
He had another.

"Listen, "Paul was saying. "Maybe you oughta do it. The
lawyer's trying to do his best for us. Let's take a ride up."

"Fuck you! I don't wanta go up there. They got all the
psychos up there."

Yet somehow he understood he couldn't resist, and when
an unmarked department car pulled up, he got in quietly.

The doctor looked to him like the "before" part of a
Charles Atlas ad: short, skinny, big glasses. They talked
for half an hour—and the doctor wanted him to spend the
night! Pete stormed out of the office screaming for Paul.

"You tell 'em . . . you tell 'em I'm not staying here."
The words came out as if he might choke. "Tell 'em they
shouldn't even try." He looked pathetically at his friend.
"Don't . . . don't let them do this, Paul. Please don't let
it happen . . ."

And Paul, who had taken his share of madmen to Bellevue, felt truly helpless. Had his partner, his "brother,"
become one of them? It was the worst of dreams.

"Pete," he said softly. "It's late, it's a long drive home.
Maybe it makes sense to spend the night."

"No way! No way in the world!" Pete's voice turned from
outrage to a desperate whine. "Don't let them do this,
Paul . . . please Paul . . . Please!"

"Wait here." Paul walked into the doctor's office, and as

the small bespectacled man listened, he explained hurriedly that Pete was scheduled for an interview with the department staff psychologist the next day. Could Bellevue wait? He promised to stay close to Pete. And as he talked, he realized he'd gotten Pete *into* this. He had to protect his friend one more time.

"If he feels safe with you," the doctor observed carefully, "it will probably be all right. Stay with him, keep him from becoming agitated. Be sure he goes to tomorrow's interview."

"I'm Police Officer Schlossberg," the short stocky man said gently. "Who are you?"

"I'm Police Officer Bon Viso." Pete tried desperately to seem relaxed. Visiting a therapist humiliated and frightened him. But it helped enormously that the doctor was a cop.

"Come into my office," the doctor said. He projected reassurance. He would help. And while Pete knew he wasn't crazy, he knew he needed help. That much he understood. So far, so good.

The conversation slipped easily into Pete's life: Helen, Pete's drinking habits, his early police career. Was he happy with Helen? Pete said he was. Did he see other women? Pete lied that he did not. Did he want to? Pete lied again. The boy—now four months old—was Pete ever jealous? "Not that I know of . . ." What did Pete mean? Well, he might be jealous without realizing it, but he didn't . . . think so. They talked of The Smith housing project and Pete's childhood. Did he drink often? Pete described his bar and the wine rack. Did he ever drink *alone?* I drink with my friends, Pete insisted.

The doctor asked Pete how he felt about being a police officer. Pete recalled his teen-age decision to become one. He talked of his trainee assignments, of the Ninth Precinct —and finally of the hated Fifth Precinct security job. Did he feel the department treated him well? The department treated him "okay," Pete said. What about the old head-quarters assignment? It was punishment, Pete admitted. Had he tried to return to the street? Pete described his attempts to talk to various bosses. How he'd watched other members of the Dozen leave.

He admitted he'd become bitter.

He described "the incident," lying that Paul was not in the building when it happened. He'd said the same thing to the Internal Affairs investigators the previous week.

How would he feel about seeing a therapist? Pete wouldn't mind. He wouldn't mind if it helped him within the department. The cop-therapist nodded. Would Pete mind sitting in the office a few minutes longer while he made some arrangements?

"Is it all right," Pete asked, "if I wait outside with my partner?"

The doctor reacted to this without visible surprise. "Why don't you want to be in here?" he asked softly.

"Uh, no special reason," Pete said. "I'd just rather be with my partner." He stopped nervously. "I don't like to be alone. He's alone out there. I'd just rather be with him."

An assistant gave Pete a list of Long Island clinics, saying that the department would pay for the visits. It was undersood that he *would* attend.

Odd voices, clicking sounds. They were tapping his phone!

He didn't know how it worked, but he'd seen enough movies to assume that a bad tap, clumsily connected, left behind voices, buzzing, clicking. This is *really* crazy, he thought. And he called Paul.

"I'll be at Pappy's Bar in Lindenhurst," he blurted out. "Call me there in half an hour—don't call me from your house. Go outside and use a public telephone." Paul started to say something, and Pete cut him off.

Pete jumped in his car. He wore the beaded medallion over his shirt. He needed to talk to Paul—he needed a gun, and he couldn't be overheard.

It was late afternoon, and the dark bar was nearly empty. Pete checked the pay phone (it worked) and ordered a beer. He noticed an old drunk stumbling back and forth between the bar and bathroom, stopping people. Pete stepped away and moved to the pool table. The drunk followed him; he moved again. Then the old man noticed Pete's medallion. He reached for it, lunging as Pete pulled away, grabbing and ripping the necklace.

Pete nearly exploded in the darkness. He reached for the man and threw him against the wall, banging the bobbing head against it. He shoved the old man back into his seat at the bar, taking what was left of his medallion back.

"Listen, he's sorry," another man at the bar said. "He's been here all day. He's just drunk."

Pete turned as if he had a weapon in his hand. "Get this fucking bastard outa here," he screamed, "or I'm gonna kill him!" The man hurriedly coaxed his friend into leaving. The phone rang.

"What's the matter?" Paul began.

"This motherfucker just ripped my medallion off!" Pete

shouted, mystifying Paul completely. "I'm gonna kill him!"
Pete held the ruptured necklace as he talked. Tiny beads
fell to the floor.

"All right, all right . . . calm down," Paul interjected.
"Now: why didn't you wanta talk on your phone?"

"It's tapped."

Paul saw no point in arguing. Besides—he suddenly decided—it might be true!

"What did you wanta talk about?" he asked cautiously.

"I need a handgun, something I can carry," Pete said in
a low voice. "Can you rustle one up?"

"I'll see what I can do," Paul said, talking slowly, as
remotely as possible. "I'll call you, uh, tonight or tomorrow."

Clutching the medallion, which dripped black and white
beads as he walked to the car, Pete sped home. He couldn't
wait for Paul. He carried his .20 gauge semi-automatic
shotgun into the garage and cut the barrel off with a hack-
saw, fashioning a mobster's sawed-off shotgun. He practiced
carrying it under a trenchcoat. He drew and dry-fired. He
was very proud. He could take out ten men if they came at
him.

For the occasion of his first reinstatement hearing, Pete
attached a leather thong to the handle of a triangular-
bladed butcher's knife and looped the thong around his
shoulder, letting the knife hang under his arm. He planned
to throw it at the trial commissioner if things went badly.
He'd practiced heaving it into a tree for three days.

"Don't fuck around," Paul said angrily when he heard
about the knife. They were entering the building. "You'll
get us killed."

"I'll get him right between the eyes," Pete smiled, staring at the elevator's walls.

"The cops up there will shoot both of us."

"If he don't restore us, I'll get him."

Paul was having some trouble taking this seriously. "Look, if we don't get restored today, we'll get restored next week, okay?" Pause. "What about our families if we get killed."

The hearing was indeed hostile: no respect, no affection —no reinstatement. The trial commissioner looked down from his bench at one cop who was defiant, which was bad enough; and at another who told ghost stories, which was worse. He had no intention of restoring them to active duty, none. The department can *terminate* you, he warned sternly. The offenses were clear: an unauthorized shooting, covering it up, conduct unbecoming police officers. At the very least, Officers Bon Viso and Rossi must admit what they did. Maybe *then*.

In the middle of the hearing Paul lost his temper. He started to walk out—and saw Pete reaching inside his sports jacket. "Don't do anything foolish," he whispered, moving close to his partner. He stayed next to him until the hearing was over.

"It should have dawned on me," Paul said years later, "that whatever was going on inside his head was bigger than the police department." Paul stopped and looked up. "Even if they fired him, it was only a job. But I admit it, I *still* thought his trouble with the department was more serious than his illness."

So Paul concentrated on getting them back into the department.

The next day he telephoned the department chaplain, who was almost hostile. "They don't give out medals for shooting up police headquarters," the cleric joked.

Paul held his breath, wondering if *anyone* understood what was happening to them. Slowly, deliberately, he suggested that the situation was more serious than the chaplain might think. They needed help. Right now, on suspension, they had neither money nor medical insurance; they couldn't help themselves. They had to get back on the force to prove they were good cops. "We're cops in trouble," Paul concluded, "and the department doesn't seem to care."

The chaplain seemed genuinely troubled now. If Pete had a drinking problem, he might be able to help. But mental illness . . . well, that was beyond his reach.

"Sir, I think mental illness is at least as serious a problem as drinking," Paul replied testily.

Carefully, the chaplain agreed that it was. He'd put Paul in touch with someone who might be able to help.

A politician, Paul thought bitterly.

But the following day, a sergeant from Employee Relations called. Would Paul care to talk about his and Pete's situation? It was the first light in a very dark sky. Pete was slipping into obvious insanity. The department was fading away. And all the while, both men were enduring the shame which clouds any cop's suspension; the family questions, newspaper headlines, pressure from all sides. Only Paul's stiff-backed ability to focus on the problem at hand kept him going. He worked steadily, riding his anger coolly, calmly hating everyone who opposed him. He was goddam stubborn—it was all that got him through.

And finally, he had an inspector to talk to. He was unsure how it had been arranged, perhaps by the chaplain, perhaps by the new lawyer (they'd fired the Irishman and gotten an Italian), but at last he had the feeling that someone would listen. He arrived promptly for his appointment and talked at length of Pete's illness, what he'd seen, their suspension, the unfairness of it. And the short, graying inspector—Paul decided he was a no-bullshit-type-person—proposed a simple solution.

Tell the truth, the inspector said.

Make a "corrected statement" to Internal Affairs, and something will be arranged. The department understands that you felt a need to protect your partner. There will be penalties; you have to understand that. But you will be reinstated. So will he.

Paul realized he had no choice. Silence meant the department would ultimately fire both of them. Haltingly, he agreed to make whatever statements were necessary. A meeting with the trial commissioner was scheduled. It would take the place of a formal "trial," and Paul would be the only witness.

A week later, Lieutenant "Red Eye" waited outside the hearing room, still in his trench coat. He demanded to know what Paul would say. And when Paul told him, he was angry.

"That's not the story," the lieutenant raged. "You tell a lie in there, and you'll be fired!"

Paul stared angrily at his inquisitor for what he hoped would be the last time. "Lieutenant," he said with a tight mouth, "I swear to God I'm telling the truh."

"A lot of things don't add up."

"I can't help it. This is the truth, and this is the story I'm gonna tell inside, whatever happens." Paul turned and walked through the door badly shaken, wondering what the lieutenant really knew.

May 2nd, 1974: during the three weeks since his suspension, Pete had moped darkly around the house, carrying his sawed-off shotgun, watching shadows. And sometimes shooting at them. He felt entombed. The phone rang.

"I've got good news," Paul said excitedly. "It looks like they'll reinstate us! They want you down here!"

Pete's police shield, his gun, his paycheck: he saw them in a delicious fantasy. He shouted the good news to Helen and ran to the shower, scrubbing excitedly. He dressed quickly, jumped in his car and flew into the city. I can carry a gun legally again! he exulted. He was almost singing. I've got protection again! He ran into departmental headquarters and pumped Paul's hand joyously. Inside the departmental hearing room a smiling trial commissioner passed the judgment he desperately wanted to hear. Having reviewed the facts of the case, the commissioner decreed, he had decided to reinstate Rossi and Bon Viso to the uniformed force. There would be restrictions: Rossi would be on probation for six months, Bon Viso would be assigned to "restricted" duty.

All Pete remembered of that moment was an almost

hysterical happiness, as if a cloud had split open to pour out champagne. He was born again; he had life itself in his hands.

CHAPTER 16

THEY had given him a pink identification card which made it impossible to carry a gun. He resolved to hide his disappointment. It was enough to see his shield again; he was sure the gun and street duty would follow. For he planned to obey the department's rules to the letter.

He was assigned to a special office now. He was part of what was jocularly called "the rubber gun squad." A sergeant processed his papers and sent him to the Records and Information command after learning he had bookkeeping skills.

Pete arrived in a vast windowless hall. He saw half a hundred clerks hunched over ancient desks shuffling papers under the watchful eye of a white-haired civil service clerk, a woman. She was friendly enough. She took him to an area cluttered with storage bins and huge piles of duplicate arrest sheets. She explained that Pete was to sort the sheets by borough and precinct, then file them in the bins. When he'd filled a bin, he was to stuff them into an envelope for delivery to the mailroom.

"Take your time," the woman smiled. "Just get things in the right place."

A copying machine hummed and flashed about 10 feet away. Pete looked at the bins and at the paper and the noisy machine, and he knew it wouldn't work. His head hurt almost immediately. He went to the men's room. He made a dozen trips to the bathroom that day. The next day, he spent even more time away from the bins. It bothered him that the room had no windows.

At the day's end, the woman told him to return to the special office. She was polite and very low-key about it. Pete didn't realize he'd been rejected. He thought he was needed somewhere else.

They sent him to the payroll office next, which he liked. It had windows, and the captain in charge let him work a slightly different shift to make his commute easier. But two weeks later, the captain needed extra men to work on a special problem, and he assigned Pete to it, sending him to a small windowless room on the tenth floor. The headaches began. Pete decided to take a couple of days off. He couldn't find any UF-28 forms, which the department requires for personal days; he went home anyway. The captain sent him back to the special office.

"Pete?"

A bearded man in a rumpled tweed suit walked into the clinic's waiting room. Pete stood up shakily.

"I'm Doctor Samuelson," the therapist said, extending his hand. Pete followed the doctor up a flight of stairs and through a corridor. He hadn't wanted to come. He'd canceled the first appointment, making a second one only when the clinic called and prodded him. Just *being* here was an admission of something deeply frightening, something he didn't want to confront. He was in full possession of his faculties. He *knew* that. Insanity was a weakness, a stigma.

Yet he talked with Dr. Samuelson for nearly an hour, and he was surprised to find it easy, almost pleasant. He told the doctor of his parents, and of his childhood. He talked of Rose's father who had died in the state hospital, of his marriage. The doctor was curious as to why Pete had let his hair and mustache grow so long. Was he trying to change his identity? Pete was shocked at the idea—but he thought it might be true! The doctor asked about his marriage. Did he see other women? Pete lied. Negative references to his moral character might get back to the department. Besides, he was embarrassed.

They talked of Victorio Sanchez. Gently, the doctor guided Pete through a discussion of reality and imagination. Sanchez, after all, did exist. That was real. How did Pete feel about him? What did Pete think he represented? How did he feel about departmental records which placed Sanchez in jail when Pete saw him on the street? Pete tried to change the subject. Yes, he knew the department had located Sanchez in jail, but . . .

The hour ended. The doctor asked how he felt about his

visit. Would he mind coming back? Pete felt strangely at ease. Yes, he would come back. He would be glad to.

"Whatta we gonna do with you?" the restricted duty sergeant asked. "We got you two nice jobs, the best offices around." Pete shrugged, and the sergeant screwed up his face and looked at a master list. "Try the auto squad," he said. "We gotta couple of guys up there. Nobody's been sent back." And this time, the job looked very good indeed. There were windows and telephones. He was assigned to a telephone-answering and record-keeping job, helping a detective who chased stolen cars and trucks.

"We have a nice office here," the portly supervising sergeant said when Pete arrived. "Everybody gets along." The sergeant looked at Pete. "By the way, guys come up here on restricted duty for a lot of reasons. I'm curious, you know?"

"I'm the guy that shot up Maurice Nadjari's office."

The sergeant suddenly remembered that Pete's job description required a short conference with a supervising captain. It was procedure. He took Pete into the office of a lean young captain with close-cropped brown hair. The captain seemed easy. He asked why Pete had just now arrived at the auto squad, since he'd been on restricted duty for two weeks.

Pete talked of his previous jobs—no windows. It drove him "a little crazy."

The captain got up from his seat. "What's this about windows?" he said calmly, easily, as he walked to his open window—they were ten stories up—and closed it. It was the middle of May, 1974, a hot day.

"I like looking outside," Pete said. "I like fresh air."

The captain returned to his desk. "How do you feel about the Nadjari incident now?"

"I feel great." Pause. "Uh, just one thing, captain." Another pause. "Don't leave your gun lying around, okay?"

Pete watched the older cop blush. "I was kidding," he said, walking out.

Restricted duty cops were required to display their I.D. pink cards on a pocket clip. Pete thought it was bad enough to be half a cop without wearing the embarrassing badge, so he rarely did. But from other men on restricted duty, he found that guns were taken away for a variety of reasons, many harmless. One cop had recurring dizzy spells after a motorcycle accident. The department confiscated his weapon so he wouldn't lose it if he happened to faint in public. Other restricted cops had been injured on duty and couldn't have defended themselves in a street emergency. And there were alcoholics on probation, lots of them.

But none of this helped. He *missed* the gun. There was no way to pretend otherwise.

Still, the auto squad was a sympathetic, easy assignment. Pete worked at a "field operations" desk, taking calls, logging in reports of stolen autos and trucks. He had time to call his mother, his wife, Marge, Paul. He arranged luncheon dates, he gossiped. And he played his little game: each phone call was for him. Soon enough, it happened.

The first call was simply blank: no voice. He let it pass. The department's switchboard fouled up often enough. He ignored the second and third calls. Then other cops began to get his calls, which were blank by the time he picked up. His irritation was mounting. Then he received three blank calls in one day, no voice, no breathing . . . just silence.

"You motherfucker!" he screamed the third time, slamming down the receiver. He bolted for the bathroom.

When he returned, the sergeant called him over.

Pete told the sergeant about Victorio Sanchez, explaining that the gunman had taunted him on the telephone before. Would Pete like a desk away from the telephones, the sergeant asked? Pete thanked him: no, not yet. If the calls continued, he said politely, maybe then.

They continued. He was taken off the field operations desk and given filing to do.

Crossing the city line a few days after that, Pete realized that Sanchez was behind him. The gunman was driving a blue Dodge, scowling over the wheel. Pete had to keep him away from police headquarters! He pulled up to a phone booth.

"I've gotta problem, Sarge," he said hurriedly. "I need the day off."

"Pete, we're short today," the sergeant answered just as quickly.

"Sarge, I hadda car accident," Pete pleaded. "There's no way I can get in there."

"Get in as fast as you can," the sergeant said, hanging up.

Sanchez seemed to have disappeared. Pete jumped into his car, aiming at downtown Manhattan. He saw Sanchez behind him again! He slammed on his brakes, hoping the gunman would crash into him. Sanchez drove around him deftly. Pete pulled off the road, and the gunman disappeared again. Now Pete drove to Central Park and walked slowly, carefully into the woods. He had no gun. But he had his butcher knife, wedged into his sock as if in an ankle holster.

Pete walked through the park all day, lurking behind trees, waiting, watching.

At six o'clock, Pete walked to a phone booth and called Helen, who apparently had talked to his office.

"Are you all right?" she blurted out. "Where've you been?"

He told her about the gunman.

"He's still around?" she asked incredulously. It had been almost two months since the backyard shotgun incident, and Helen hoped her husband was better. She told him the sergeant was threatening to list him AWOL.

The following morning the entire auto squad seemed angry. They'd called the Nassau County police department about his "accident" and found that he'd lied. Even the other restricted duty cops demanded an explanation, which Pete stubbornly refused to give. He felt he couldn't tell them about Sanchez. The sergeant refused to drop the AWOL charge, which meant Pete would have to appear before a charges and specifications hearing. The result could be suspension again, or worse.

In the weeks that followed, he walked out of the office again and again because of the telephone calls. He was called into the department's Advocate office, where a young lieutenant wasted no words—shape up or be fired! You're being given every chance, you're giving nothing back. It was July by now, the middle of a muggy summer and departmental vacations, and his hearing was scheduled for early Fall, giving him another chance. He returned to the auto squad and promised he'd "do right."

But he was beginning to realize that he didn't know what that was.

He didn't see Paul very much, and this bothered him, too. Was Paul pulling away? For a while, Paul had called almost every day. They met for lunch. They had drinks after work. But Paul was a cop again; he had been re-assigned to the Ninth, working day and evening tours, and he seemed to be doing well. He had his gun back. He had "war stories" to tell; Pete had nothing. Pete sat in his civilian clothes as they drank and became deeply afraid. Maybe Paul was bored with him? Each time they met, he asked Paul to stay in the city and have dinner or drinks with him.

Paul said he couldn't afford it now.

The problem was more complex than money. Paul's marriage had suffered enormously because of his friendship with Pete; his career had been jeopardized. He and Catherine had separated briefly. They'd resolved some of their problems through counseling and were together again. But Catherine had pointed to Pete as the symptom (if not the cause) of their problems.

Paul cared for Pete as much as ever, but below the surface of his affection—and pity—he was deeply troubled. He knew his own future lay in other directions: with his family, in uniform, *without* Pete.

He *had* to convince the doctors that he was sane, that he merited the return of his guns. He was surprised that they were only vaguely interested in his fantasies of Victorio Sanchez. He did believe they were fantasies, he told the doctor.

He didn't believe it entirely, of course.

The summer passed into August. On a Tuesday, he asked his doctor if he should make another appointment. The doctor asked Pete what *he* thought. And Pete thought he could let it go for a while. He felt very relaxed, he said. As Pete remembers it, the doctor seemed to agree. Pete didn't have to make another appointment immediately if he didn't care to, the doctor said. Pete said he'd also started to see a private psychiatrist in the city. The doctor was glad to hear that.

He didn't see the doctor for several months. By then it no longer mattered.

He found it increasingly hard to work in the auto squad. Too many distractions. The phone calls wouldn't stop; and the department charges were piling up. He felt a very thin blade pressing in: the end of his police career. He knew it would end. He couldn't admit it—he couldn't talk about it. But the blade came at him. He would be gone soon.

He decided to play tennis for relaxation. At lunchtime, he bought rackets and a can of tennis balls, and several days later, he walked into the auto squad's back room and closed the door. He began lobbing balls against the room's metal walls, which boomed in response. He worked up to a steady volley. The door opened.

"What is this?" the sergeant shouted. "Are you crazy?"

Pete threw his racket on the floor with a clatter.

"Don't you ever call me crazy!" he shouted at the older man. "I'll kill you if you do!"

The sergeant backed out quickly. Pete waited. The door opened again, and he saw several younger cops.

"Everything all right?" one asked gently. "You okay?" They left the door open. Pete walked out of it, through the office, to the bathroom. He drank a cup of coffee, and he returned to work.

The auto squad didn't understand him. They didn't understand why he had to leave when the telephones rang, why he needed so desperately to be back in the streets. The summer was nearly gone, and the charges and specifications were mounting. He felt very bad. He was done with the shrinks on Long Island. He felt he was cured. But the department seemed to be ignoring this. They would not give him his due. He would be sent away like a crippled child. Like his parents . . .

He talked vaguely of alternatives, perhaps a business. He'd run it. Paul, still on duty, would be his silent partner. He thought of starting an after-hours social club. Social clubs, of course, were usually cracker-box operations, cramped, dingy, furtive, but he figured he could show more class. Another Ninth Precinct cop who had left the force offered to come in as an active partner; and shortly after that other silent partners, all cops, approached him.

He began looking for a location and soon found a five-story river front warehouse where an old man had operated a restaurant on the second floor. The concession had closed; it was perfect. From the outside, the old warehouse seemed to be nothing more than a building scheduled for demolition. Pete decided to locate the club on the third floor, using the kitchen facilities below for parties. The old man, who was somehow connected to organized crime, talked to someone and returned with a price: $1500 up front, a thousand dollars a month after that. Pete nearly gagged. He talked to the other cops and the partners decided to offer the man a fifth of the profits instead. It was agreed. All that remained was to put in plumbing, bathrooms, a long wooden bar, and decorate the vast space. And spread the word.

The auto squad threw him out. He'd missed too many work days, wandering off after lunch, disappearing midday when telephone calls upset him. Long cups of coffee; longer sessions in the men's room. Pete seemed almost to be forcing the issue. For slowly, shakily, he'd begun to realize that serious cases of restricted duty didn't go back to the street. Men with routine injuries and mild drinking or emotional problems were given their guns again; that was all.

Now his instincts were taking over. He was summoned to a disciplinary hearing the day after he left the auto squad. He stayed home. Something in him seemed to seek the confrontation that was coming. The bureaucracy ground its teeth and went to work. Half a dozen "charges and specifications" were rolled into one angry list. The case for termination was drawn up. Pete was now given a vague sick leave and advised to call his lawyer. In a fog he wandered down to the Ninth to look for Paul. As the weeks passed, he haunted Avenue C, gossiping with Abie, playing cards in the Avenue C club, talking to Sam, the candy man. If anyone asked, he said he was on "special assignment" working on "an old case."

The people on Avenue C passed the time with Pete and thought nothing about it.

In a dream, he was at a funeral. Helen and Paul were with him; so were other friends and relatives. He walked to the casket to pay respects—and he saw himself. They'd dressed him in a dark suit, blue tie, blue shirt. He saw that his eyes were open, hands folded on his chest, fingers interlocking. And everybody around him seemed to be happy: talking, drinking, laughing. He was stunned. He backed away from the casket as if it were a hot stove. The only person missing from the funeral was Victorio Sanchez.

The trial commissioner was surprisingly sympathetic. A department lawyer had argued for immediate resuspension followed by Pete's termination. But his new lawyer, the Italian, talked convincingly of Pete's "problem." His client's emotional state had caused this erratic behavior, he declared. He needed help, not punishment. The commissioner agreed and gently assigned Pete to "sick report." It was October of 1974, and Pete was required only to remain home, answerable from time to time to department supervisors.

Pete was rarely there. Mostly, he worked on the club, which was to be called "Jack's Hideaway." He hoped that Ninth Precinct cops would flock to the old warehouse, and he hung around the precinct talking endlessly of it. His old colleagues could make or break the place. He worked long hours putting in the plumbing and building the long bar. He'd be rich, he told Helen exuberantly. The club's potential was unbounded! Helen saw that Pete was spending more and more time away from home. She became deeply troubled. Pete was slipping away from her.

Pete's final hearing was staffed by doctors. He asked the lawyer to be there—the lawyer declined. The doctors asked about the headquarters shooting. Had he really thought Sanchez would kill him? Did he understand that he was hallucinating? How did he feel?

Pete braced himself.

He'd gone through a little problem. Yes, that was true. But it was over. Pete watched them as he talked, trying to be earnest and solemn. His head bobbed as he talked, trying to be steady. He was completely cured, he insisted. He was over it. He was willing to return to fulltime duty immediately. He stopped and looked at them.

We'll let you know, the doctors said. The hearing ended.

Helen always left his mail on the kitchen table. He read it over his coffee, and that day he saw the official envelope immediately. For a moment he couldn't bring himself to open it. He was nearly done with his second cup of coffee when he finally read the letter, which confirmed what he already knew. Somehow, against all logic, he'd hoped for another result.

His "terminal leave" would begin on November 11th. On that day, or before it, Pete was ordered to report to the pension office to turn in his shield and department identification. He'd be paid for several weeks remaining vacation time. Then Pete would begin a $5000 annual "disability" pension. He wouldn't be a cop any longer.

In the truest sense of the department phrase, he'd "died."

CHAPTER 17

THE game was not in Jack's Hideaway, but in a cramped balcony above a smaller social club, behind a blue door, up a flight of stairs. The unmarked door was on a sidestreet off Second Avenue, and the stairs climbed over an empty after-hours bar whose customers would arrive about 4 A.M.

The gamblers inside were armed. Some kept their guns in holsters clipped to their belts; others wore shoulder harnesses. The game had a sense of gathering violence about it. On the table, twenty, fifty and one-hundred dollar bills were stacked and scattered about as if the men had robbed a bank. The combination of guns, greenbacks and muted violence suggested a Wild West poker game: outlaws, six shooters, cigars, whiskey, all transported through a time warp to New York's Lower East Side.

The outlaws at the table were cops.

Pete carried a pistol, too. He wanted to be able to help cops—anywhere, anytime—who might be in trouble; and he had to protect himself. Pete was not a cop now, and while most of the men at the table knew it, they said nothing, accepting him.

The men played a rough game, growling fiercely over the cards, lapsing into tense silence when big money was about to be won or lost, laughing in between, throwing out ethnic barbs which exploded scatter-shot in the small space. Since nearly every subculture in the city was represented— black, Italian, Irish, Puerto Rican—the racial slurs landed fairly evenly. The only other non-cop at the table was Louis, a local Puerto Rican wholesaler chomping solemnly on a fat cigar. He wisely stayed out of the ethnic give and take, competing only in plumage.

Hands holding the cards around the table sparkled with a profusion of pinky rings: two of glittering sapphire, a white-gold and diamond piece belonging to Louis, and Pete's two diamond-chip rings, one shaped in his initials, another forming a horse-shoe. A fifth player wore a flat-brimmed pimp's hat bedecked with pheasant feathers. Eventually, he would be the night's winner.

Before gambling, Pete always put his "financial affairs" in order. And, he hoped, his life. The table was no place for mongrel thoughts. And for that reason, he had been a little tense that day as he drove his decaying Cadillac convertible around town. He'd bought it recently, and it was a little banged up, but it was an eye-catching shiny-white car, a conversation piece among friends, part of his new image. He was wearing flared slacks, a flowered open necked shirt (gold chain showing) and a leather suburban coat as he drove uptown with the radio turned up loud.

But the inner man behind that bravado was tense. He'd fought repeatedly with Marge the previous day and night— and of course *nothing* was going well in his marriage. As a gambler, he knew that the best cards came to a steady hand. He had to straighten himself out. He filled the Cadillac's tank, took some clothes out of the cleaners, bought groceries. He drove to Rose's apartment and gave her $100 for "safe keeping."

After that, Pete had parked outside a Second Avenue bank and withdrawn two thousand dollars from a private account. He'd opened the account six weeks earlier, walking up to a bank official with a thick roll of twenties. "I'm a gambler," he told the man, who inquired nervously about the money's origin. In the following weeks, he'd doubled the amount, thanks mostly to his weekly poker games, plus winnings from gin rummy at the Avenue C club, adding an occasional prize from his bookie.

He had to win now.

Seven card stud, which involved a slow climb to a big pot, was the night's favorite game. Each hand began low: five dollar ante, initial ten and twenty dollar bets, fifty and one-hundred dollars on the later rounds, two hundred on the last card. By 10 P.M. Pete was fifteen hundred dollars down.

Across the table, a black detective nicknamed Lamont (for his slight resemblance to a TV character) had most of the money. Fat Tony, a beefy detective with an elaborate shoulder holster, sat next to Pete. Tony was throwing out most of the ethnic jabs.

On the next hand, Pete started well. He had tens underneath and a queen up. By the fifth card, the dealer delivered another queen: two and two, solid. Pete worked quickly to drive the others out, dropping a series of fifty dollar bets with his queens showing, a modest bluff.

By the seventh card, Pete had pushed all the players off the table except the cop in the flat-brimmed hat, who had nines showing. Silence settled over the circle of men. Pete dropped another fifty into the pot. If The Hat had another nine underneath, Pete was dead. But the Hat folded, giving Pete an extended sentence.

A new hand. Pete felt very good. He'd pulled four clubs in the first four cards, and he felt confident enough now to start pushing the others from the table. A second black detective had dropped out of the game entirely, and he stood behind Lamont—still the table's top money man—swilling grapefruit juice and slapping palms when Lamont won.

"I'm gonna steal it," Pete said out loud, convinced he'd begun the run he needed. He threw fifty dollars into the pot, humming to himself.

The room around them was almost totally without charm. The exposed brick walls beyond the table were pocked with white patches of broken glaze. Cheap plastic curtains hid another wall of badly peeling plaster. A half-open booth near the railing contained a smelly sink and toilet.

Two more cards came down, no clubs. Pete began to sweat. Lamont was still in. The pot already held hundreds and hundreds of Pete's dollars.

He kept the last card out of sight when it came, shuffling his hand tightly, opening it slowly.

No new clubs. Pete was armed with a sad pair of eights. Lamont had sixes showing. Pete couldn't bluff.

"Eights," he said limply, turning over his cards.

The black detective had aces underneath. He took Pete's money with long arms.

Pete was riding a particularly frightening roller coaster: dropping to a dead end stake of two hundred dollars, rising to a thousand, dropping back. He held "scared money," his savings, his seed money.

Now he was climbing again. A hand had started with kings down and a three on top, a perfect betting hand. He threw in ten dollars, played cautiously, raised another ten dollars. Small stuff. Another three on top. He started twenty dollar bets, aiming toward fifty. Danny, a graying Irishman next to him, had tens and threes, having filled a full house. Pete drew another king. He was ready for the kill, teeth clenched behind a tight smile. Kings full! He was alive again—he dropped one hundred dollars into the pot and watched Danny raise him. Wow! He matched Danny's two hundred, doubled it—and won! He was back in the game. Again, he had life.

By midnight, he'd climbed back to his original stake, but he was stalled. The cop in the flat-brimmed hat was cutting into Lamont's money, but the action seemed to be limited to the two of them. Pete, Fat Tony, Danny and Louis were struggling badly.

In the next hand, Pete had a spade flush by the sixth

card. He threw $100 into the pot. Lamont raised. Pete matched it without hesitating. On the seventh card, he threw in $200. He was surprised to see Lamont match it and raise two hundred more. Lamont was showing nines. Pete matched the $200 and raised *again*. Lamont, squeezing his cards briefly, matched it and called.

"All black," Pete said triumphantly, turning the cards over.

"Boat," answered the detective, turning over a full house. Pete's stomach came at him like a tidal wave.

He walked through the blue door into the warm spring night. He had less than two hundred dollars in his pocket. The cop in the flat-brimmed hat was carrying five thousand. The black detective was at least two thousand dollars wealthier.

Pete Bon Viso wouldn't go home tonight. He didn't go home that much anyway. He was driving Helen crazy, and he knew it. But he had to keep moving. He stayed with Marge most of the time now; Helen didn't know this. She knew that he was gone, nothing more. When she waited up for him, he explained that he'd slept at the precinct house, or at his mother's. Or at Jack's Hideaway, which was failing. Internal Affairs investigators had begun to check license plates outside the warehouse, and since cops are not officially allowed to go to unlicensed clubs, the Ninth Precinct cops had stopped coming.

The club's business, already marginal, was cut by half.

Helen watched all this from Long Island, alone with Billy. Paul, who might have been able to help, had left for an extended tour of Air Force para-rescue training. He was thousands of miles away. Pete worked nights now and slept only by day, tending bar, gambling, moving. He saw Helen once, perhaps twice a week. And they fought and cried, and she tried to be understanding. It was impossible.

Pete was still a cop, of course. He insisted on that, and he carried his gun every day. He *had* to be there if a brother was in trouble. It was his last dream of glory. And, of course, he had to protect himself against Victorio Sanchez, the man who refused to die, and who lived now like a demon inside him.

EPILOGUE

A YEAR had passed since the headquarters shooting. I'd asked Pete to take me to Sanchez's old neighborhood, and we'd made the trip downtown in the old Cadillac, whose windshield wipers malfunctioned badly in the rainy gloom of a Tuesday night. It was late spring, and the Eighth Street block of tenements where Sanchez once lived was dark and quiet. In shadows cast by street lamps, small groups of people huddled in the doorways, talking and drinking.

Pete's life had slipped even further downhill. Jack's Hideaway was dead, and he had thrown his marriage away as if it were part of a bad memory. He had no job, and he couldn't afford poker, so he lived on smaller football and baseball bets and what he could scrape together from old investments. He had given his pension to Helen. The Long Island house was a sad memory, sold earlier that spring. Helen and Billy had moved to a two-bedroom apartment in Queens.

Pete had moved in with Marge. She hadn't taken kindly to it at first, but in the end she had accepted him and his suitcase of troubles. They'd moved into a small upper east side apartment, and Pete continued the business of cutting himself off from his former life.

For all this, Pete's spirits were high as we turned onto Eighth Street. It was his way. He always tried to look good. And he insisted, as he had insisted for so long, that he fully understood the difference between fantasy and reality. The gunman *was* in jail, doing three to five years. Pete carried his gun mostly out of habit, he said.

We cruised down the block, and he pointed to Sanchez' old tenement, number 318. The building sat in a block of squalor. Across the street, a vacant warehouse smiled toothlessly at us with three floors of broken windows. A deserted synagogue stood next to it, yellow bricks filthy with age, windows shattered leaving behind needle fragments of broken blue glass.

Number 318 had been gutted by fire. A yellow "Pepsi-Groceries" sign had survived on the ground floor. A ramshackle store-front church stood next to the wreckage of the cream-brick building, inspirational messages painted on its decaying surface. Next to it was the tomato-red front of the El Arbelito social club, then another tenement (number 314) and finally a candy store with some battered garbage cans out front.

r in front of number 314 I noticed a short, chunky man

with a dark face. He was talking to two women, and he turned briefly into the street lamp's glare.

"It's *him*," Pete whispered behind me. "It's Sanchez!"

A bad joke, I thought.

"I tell you it's him!" Pete whispered urgently.

"It isn't funny, Pete."

"No"—the voice beside me shifted slightly—"it's him all right." Again, Pete moved in the seat.

I watched the man beneath the street lamp, waiting for this odd moment to resolve itself. Beside me, Pete had moved again. From his nervousness, it was clear he was frightened.

I did not see the hand, which had dropped to the dead metal of his gun in the darkness.

"Blackie!" Pete's voice called shakily from the car. "Hey, Vic! Can we talk to you for a minute?"

The man standing by the tenement stoop wore a hooded gray sweatshirt, brown corduroy pants, dark sneakers. He had a round face, small eyes and tight curly hair; he turned curiously. Then he said something to one of the women, shoved his hands into the sweatshirt pockets and walked over. He probably assumed he had no choice. Two white men in a car could only be cops.

"How ya doin'?" Pete asked as if seeing an old friend.

I watched the short man with dumb curiosity. He seemed relaxed, but there was an old glint in his eyes, which monitored us like periscopes.

And Pete was reaching for his gun again. Only my presence stopped him.

"When'd you get out?" Pete was introducing me now.

"Last November," the short man said, shaking my hand through the window. It happened to be the same month Pete had left the department. Sanchez looked past me. He'd served 28 months in jail; he was on parole now.

"Hey, you . . . you did me a favor, you know?" Sanchez leaned against the car. "I was . . . uh . . . excuse the expression . . . fucked *up,* you know?"

"Whatta you doing now?" Pete had assumed a cop's demeanor. "You doin' any drugs?"

"No, man." Sanchez seemed almost insulted. "All I do is drink."

"You doing methadone?"

"No, that shit is worse. I did it for three days, and I quit."

The rain had increased its pressure. I asked Sanchez if he wanted to get in. On the surface the conversation seemed congenial enough, and I wanted to interview him.

He politely declined the offer, raising the hood of his sweatshirt. The rain fell thickly.

"You had enough?" Pete whispered, tapping me on the shoulder, his voice clearly quavering. I paid no attention and suggested we leave the car and stand in a doorway. The ex-cop and the ex-gunman agreed, reluctantly.

"I'm not goin' back to that life again," Sanchez was saying in the tenement hall. "I got a wife and two kids, and my sister lives around here, so I come to visit sometimes. But I don't stay, you know? This neighborhood is bad— too much trouble. I gotta bike. I ride to Central Park, other places. I go all around."

The rain had let up slightly. Pete's "ghost" stood with

his back against the door, keeping it slightly ajar. And Pete stood stiffly off to one side of the passageway . . . tense, withdrawn.

"You working?" he asked. The words came in quick, low tones.

"Little of this, little of that." Sanchez moved his hand toward the door. "Some plumbing jobs, some carpentry things. I'm seeing a man next week about cutting cloth." He looked at Pete nervously. "Pays good, maybe $85 a week, more when you get into the union."

In the yellow light of the narrow, dirty hallway, the gunman remembered something else.

"They sent some people up to talk to me," he tilted his head to one side. "Something happened to you guys, right? Two lieutenants showed me your picture . . . asked if I'd seen you when I was on furlough, went to your house or something." Pause. Pete stiffened. "I said, whatta you talking about? I never saw you. I was on leave Christmas, 1973—seven days—I didn't see you. I didn't see you at all."

Pete stood by the wall staring at the short man, who continued to talk.

"Funny, you know? I *did* see you this weekend. Goin' into some club."

"You saw me?" Pete was like a wire badly stretched. He leaned forward. "Did I see you?"

"No." The short man edged even closer to the door. "You wouldn't see me, you know?"

Clearly, it was time to leave. Pete made a short, jerky motion toward the hallway door, and Sanchez and I walked out behind him. The rain had turned to dark mist, and the short, chunky man stood under the street lamp, hands in his pockets, waiting. Suddenly, he was one of thousands of poor people on New York's Lower East Side, nothing more. He watched as we entered the Cadillac and drove away.

"Jesus! If I'd seen him the other night," Pete said suddenly, "I would've put six into him. I know it!"

He turned a corner, hands clenched at the wheel. "I could take him out *any* time now. They'd have to call it self-defense." Pete was talking very fast. "He threatened my life. There were witnesses. I could take him out."

We sat in a bar called Sobossek's, a sometime cop hangout. Sanchez was minutes behind us, and Pete was slumped in his seat.

"People with mental illness are weak," he said, nodding at his glass. "My analysis is that I became frightened and weak; I allowed his threats to take over my mind. What I don't understand is, I've gotten plenty of other threats. Why *him?*" Pete shifted uncomfortably. "To hallucinate someone is trying to kill you, it's obviously a weakness."

A cop came in the door and waved to Pete. "When I realized I was weak, I was . . . disappointed in myself. I've thought about this. And I feel the only way to bring myself back up to my standards is to cure myself." He stopped. "Or kill myself."

He stopped again. "And I hope I'm curing myself."

The cop who came in, burly and blond, walked over. Pleasantries were exchanged, and he wandered off. It was after midnight and business was slow.

Pete slumped into his seat again. "I wouldn't let them confine me, I knew that. And I knew that if I continued on my course of hallucinating and shooting things up, I'd eventually be confined somewhere." He looked up. "God forbid if I should ever shoot somebody by mistake, I'd be confined. But I would make sure that never happened. I'd probably try to kill myself if they attempted to confine me—so maybe I threaten myself by carrying the gun. I scare myself into straightening out."

He smiled at what was coming. "I hope I never kill myself. But it would make a good end to your story." The smile faded quickly.

"I still think I'm a cop. The difference now is that I don't get a paycheck, I get a pension." He thought about this, and nodded to himself. "I go down to the precinct—I've lost some friends down there, I guess—and I sit around and I listen to the guys tell their war stories and what happened on the job. And not being able to contribute doesn't exactly hurt, but it leaves me out. I can feel myself drifting away. So one reason I carry a gun is . . . is because if I ever see a cop in trouble, I'm right there."

The bar is quiet now, and we've stood up to leave.

"Police officers are very close. They look out for each other."

A year has passed since that conversation, and very little has changed. Paul returned from his Air Force training and he works in a precinct on the upper west side. He calls Pete, and they see each other occasionally, and they talk of old times. Paul's marriage is stronger, but he sometimes misses Pete. "I think about what we had," he says simply. "I'm driving. I'm flying in a plane, I've got some time on my hands. I think about it." He is clearly older.

"The fun is gone. It's a job now, and I feel the time passing. I miss the fun we had." He stops. "I miss it a lot."

Helen and Pete are divorced. She and Billy live in the Queens apartment. She lives quietly, dating occasionally. On workdays, she leaves her son, who has grown into a feisty toddler, at her mother's where Pete visits him. On holidays he brings presents to the Queens apartment for both Helen and Billy.

Marge Riley, meanwhile, has become a steady, reassuring force in Pete's life. She works by day and spends time with her children in the afternoons, and she stays close to Pete at night.

And Pete has no job except gambling. But he has dreams. He is in motion, as always—and for now, the gun is gone, thanks partly to Marge's quiet insistence. Pete drives his aging Cadillac downtown to see Rose, who berates and pampers him with her fierce love, and then he drives uptown to see friends, then to Brooklyn to see his son. He hums a tune and smokes his big cigars.

But no one can say when the phone will ring again.